THE DEADLY 1940 ALAMO TRAIN CRASH

JUAN P. CARMONA AND
TAYLOR SEAVER DE LA FUENTE

THE
History
PRESS

Published by The History Press
Charleston, SC
www.historypress.com

First published 2024

Manufactured in the United States

ISBN 9781467155106

Library of Congress Control Number: 2023946783

Notice: The information in this book is true and complete to the best of our knowledge. It is offered without guarantee on the part of the authors or The History Press. The authors and The History Press disclaim all liability in connection with the use of this book.

CONTENTS

CONTENTS

ACKNOWLEDGEMENTS

This book began as a project in Donna High School's Mexican American Studies class of 2020–21, in which the students produced a four-episode podcast about the event and its impact on the community. The students conducted primary source research through digital archives and newspapers. What is amazing is that we were able to do all the research and produce most of the podcast via online meetings, for it was the middle of the pandemic, and we were all pleasantly surprised by its final version. We would also like to acknowledge the help of the Ramon family and Alex Oyoque of the City of Alamo Museum for all the assistance they provided in telling this story. Finally, we would like to acknowledge the assistance of Ms. Nicholle Moreno, whose help in cataloging and organizing our documents allowed for easy accessibility in the writing of this book.

To properly credit the students behind the podcast *The Alamo Train Crash of 1940*, their names are listed below:

Victoria Aguinaga

Selma Alvarez

Danielle Ayala

Emily Bernabe

Marlen Garcia Calvo

Aron Cancino

Reynaldo Cazares Jr.

Kiara Chavez

Vanessa Coronado

Joselyn Dominguez-Arenas

Mario Gonzalez Jr.

Nilse Granados

Sarahi Guerra

Kendra Guerrero

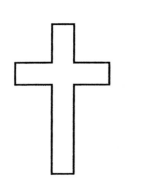

DEDICATION OF

TEXAS HISTORICAL MARKER

FOR

ALAMO TRAIN-TRUCK COLLISION

sponsored by
TEXAS HISTORICAL COMMISSION
HIDALGO COUNTY HISTORICAL COMMISSION
CITY OF ALAMO

| Saturday, April 13, 2002 | Tower Road at Railway |
| 10:00 A.M. | Alamo, Texas |

The pamphlet from the historical marker dedication ceremony. *Courtesy of the City of Alamo Museum.*

Inscription on Marker

1940 TRAIN-TRUCK COLLISION
ON MARCH 14, 1940, AT THIS CROSSING OF TOWER ROAD AND THE MISSOURI PACIFIC RAIL LINE, OCCURRED AN AUTOMOBILE ACCIDENT RESULTING IN THE MOST FATALITIES ON A TEXAS HIGHWAY IN THE 20TH CENTURY. AN ONCOMING TRAIN COLLIDED WITH A TRUCK CARRYING MORE THAN 40 AGRICULTURAL WORKERS, KILLING 34 OF THE WORKERS, WHO RANGED IN AGE FROM TEN TO 48. THE NEIGHBORING CITRUS PACKING PLANT SERVED AS HEADQUARTERS FOR RESCUE OPERATIONS. THE TRAGEDY AFFECTED MANY LIVES IN THE ALAMO COMMUNITY AND ACROSS THE RIO GRANDE VALLEY, RESULTING IN RENEWED ATTENTION TO SAFETY ISSUES SURROUNDING RAILROAD CROSSINGS AND THE TRANSPORTATION OF AGRICULTURAL WORKERS.

2002

City of Alamo Officials

Mayor	Rudy Villarreal
Mayor Pro-tem	Robert de la Garza
City Commissioner	Diana Martinez
City Commissioner	Jesus "Jesse" Vela, Jr.
City Commissioner	Victor Perez
City Manager	Luciano Ozuna, Jr.
City Secretary	Margot Saenz
City Fire Chief	Rolando Espinoza

The City of Alamo and the Hidalgo County Historical Commission appreciates the role of Crest Fruit Company and its President Val Gersting in marker placement.

PROGRAM

Color Guard	PSJA ROTC
Buglers	Robert Ortiz
	Gladys De La Cerda
Master of Ceremonies	Dr. R.E. Norton, Hidalgo County Historical Comm.
Invocation	Rev. Luis L. Brum
Welcome	Mayor Rudy Villarreal
Introductions	Mayor Rudy Villarreal
	Ann Washington - HCHC
	Joe Ramon - families
Historic statements	Mayor Rudy Villarreal
	Joe Ramon
Unveiling of marker	Santos Rosa
	Rolando Espinoza
Reading of marker inscription	Gerardo Rosa
Benediction	Rev. Luis L. Brum

Following the ceremony, attendees are invited to the Alamo Community Building for visitation and refreshments.

Hidalgo County Officials

Hidalgo County Judge	Eloy Pulido
Hidalgo County Treasurer	Norma Garcia
Hidalgo County Commissioner Pct. 1	Sylvia Handy
Hidalgo County Commissioner Pct. 2	Hector Palacios
Hidalgo County Commissioner Pct. 3	Joe Flores
Hidalgo County Commissioner Pct. 4	Oscar Garza

Officers Hidalgo County Historical Commission

Chairperson	Ann Washington
Secretary	Marj Johnson
Treasurer	Virginia Haynie Gause

ACKNOWLEDGEMENTS

Clarissa Helguera
Ingrid Iracheta
Madison Lugo
Audree Martinez
Maribel Ortiz De La Cruz
Kenia Perez
Hailey Quintana

Natasha Ramirez
Damian Rodriguez
John Rodriguez
David Santana
Taylor Seaver
Jackeline Villegas
Vivianne Zavala

INTRODUCTION

BY JUAN CARMONA

In America, and indeed throughout the world, we have heroes, soldiers, activists and first responders, but to me, my favorite and often most dismissed heroes are the people who quietly keep our country moving forward unbeknownst to us. They never stand up to be recognized, nor do they beat their chests; they do what they do because it must be done so that their families can survive. What more noble effort could there truly be? I remember an old western, *The Magnificent Seven*, in which the children of farmers call their fathers cowards to one of the gunslingers who has come to protect the town from an outlaw. The gunfighter promptly grabs one up and spanks him, explaining that their fathers are the true heroes because they carry a heavy weight on their shoulders, a weight called responsibility— something the responsibility-free life of a gunfighter has not the guts for.

In that one scene, you see the extreme contrast between what we have always been taught to perceive as a hero and what a hero truly is, for we usually define tough as in a sense being violent or exuding the air of potential violence. America's list of heroes is littered with names of violent men. Violence is usually done in wartime and therefore in a military sense. However, you can also add to the list people like Wild Bill Hickok, Wyatt Earp, Jack Johnson and Muhammad Ali, and we also have comic book heroes like Spiderman and Superman. What this group all has in common is that they use force for good and that makes them heroes. However, as the gunfighter played by Charles Bronson points out, this toughness that they wear on their faces, their stances, their walk and their stare, hides a fear of real-life responsibility.

Gunfighters, boxers and soldiers all exist in a violent world unto their own, a world where they are removed from the day-to-day life of most of the public. It is a hyper-reality in which their existence is the fight; they are fighting to not be in that normal world of struggle. In fact, most of these men know that struggle. They live in a way where their trade exerts almost total control of their lives. It is them and their opponent or the enemy, a very small world indeed. These fights can be minutes, maybe hours or, sometimes in the case of war, years. Now I must add that I see these men as heroes as well; their sacrifice and valor should never be in question. Nevertheless, there are heroes who assume great struggle or responsibility, and these are the ones who deserve better recognition. They are my true heroes, and I cannot say it better than the scriptwriter in *The Magnificent Seven*:

> *Don't you ever say that again about your fathers because they are not cowards. Do you think I am brave because I carry a gun? Well, your fathers are much braver because they carry responsibility—for you, your brothers, your sisters, and your mothers. And this responsibility is like a big rock that weighs a ton. It bends and it twists them until finally, it buries them under the ground. And there's nobody says they have to do this. They do it because they love you and because they want to. I have never had this kind of courage. Running a farm, working like a mule every day with no guarantee anything will ever come of it. This is bravery.*
> —*Charles Bronson as Bernardo O'Reilly in* The Magnificent Seven

I grew up, as we all did, with people like this, people who worked every day coming home hiding the pain in their hands and in their backs, the humiliation they endure in and out of the workplace, the looks they get as they are being driven to and from the worksite. For women, there is the added reality of sexual harassment and assault. Yet they all persevere; they do it so that they can provide a better life for their family and so that their children can have full bellies, light to do their homework, money to buy clothes for school and, nowadays, internet.

These people who have our undying love, they were the first faces that showed us what true love is. We are forever in their debt, and their sacrifice should be on the same lines as the previously mentioned heroes. They allow us to be who we are. It is to these human beings who bear the horrible weight of responsibility with a smile for their children that this book is truly dedicated. Those who were lost on that horrible day were on that truck to fulfill their responsibility to others.

PART I

BACKGROUND

BRIEF HISTORY OF THE RIO GRANDE

VALLEY AND THE CITY OF ALAMO

In what is now South Texas, specifically the city of Alamo, colonization by the Spanish and the existence of Native inhabitants are crucial in understanding the continuing culture of the Rio Grande Valley (RGV) known today. When discussing the city of Alamo before the 1900s, much of the historical information available is in the history of the general area of the Rio Grande Valley before borders, counties or towns were established. It is important to remember that the Native presence in South Texas was strong, and this land was not yet split between ruling countries; but that is not to say that through the progression of history, the peoples and cultures that would colonize the Rio Grande Valley would not leave a cultural mark and legacy or constitute their own societies and cultures.

Long before the settlement by the Spanish commenced, Native peoples, such as the Coahuiltecans, Carrizo Comecrudo and Karankawas, lived and thrived throughout the harsh terrain and climate of South Texas. Like the present cultural legacy of the Spanish, the history of Native populations in South Texas is instrumental in understanding the entirety of RGV life. Culturally speaking, South Texas was not made up of a monolithic social or cultural identity and still isn't; instead, it is marked by the various groups of Native peoples. In what is described as a "triangularly shaped region," from the Guadalupe River to Eagle Pass and through the Mexican states of Coahuila, Nuevo León and Tamaulipas, there were several societies. The Rio Grande delta and regions south of it were described as highly dense in Indian populations by explorer Álvar Núñez Cabeza de Vaca throughout

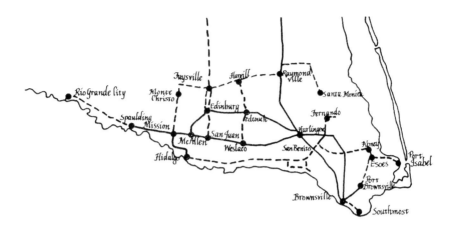

Map of early railroad lines of the Rio Grande Valley. *Courtesy of Frank Jacobsen.*

his 1530 journeying. In fact, author Florence Johnson Scott discusses what is the first attempt at exploration of the Rio Grande by Alonso Álvarez de Pineda in 1519, in which numerous Indian villages were encountered along the banks of the river. Therefore, the South Texas region was not desolate and, in fact, was populated by many different peoples.[1]

The area that would become known as the Rio Grande Valley was designated as Nuevo Santander and would continue with that designation until the Mexican-American War of 1848. The beginning of Spanish exploration throughout what is now Texas and northern Mexico created tension between the Native peoples and the Spanish. The effort to conquer/colonize the Rio Grande Valley was led by José de Escandón, a Spanish subject, military officer and devout Catholic. Escandón's organization efforts became popular among the people of northern Mexico, especially those interested in the land. Ranchers were interested in Nuevo Santander, as it proposed good land for cattle. Those who were impoverished believed this land was a new opportunity; traders thought of it as a new area to advertise and sell; and to those of political importance, new land meant new ventures of power. That being said, land grants would become of utmost importance when discussing what is now the Lower Rio Grande Valley and northern Mexico. These early settlements would go on to be cities in the modern RGV.

Ranching would remain the dominant industry up until the late 1800s, when a series of downward turns plagued the South Texas ranchers. The earliest use for South Texas cattle was for "hide and tallow" factories that sprang up all along with the ranches of South Texas. This trade was one of the primary means of making money off the cattle trade in Texas from 1840 to 1880. "Hide and tallow" was an industry that was readily suited to the distant frontier of South Texas, especially before the establishment of the railroads. What was sold was the hide of the cattle, which was boiled off and cured, plus the horns, each of which would earn the cattleman a profit. The reduction of cattle to hide and tallow allowed for the cattlemen to transport their wares via the Gulf Coast, aboard ship, instead of attempting the difficult journey of driving the cattle up north. This industry became so profitable that during two especially cold winters in 1872 and 1873, some cattlemen all but depleted their stock.[2]

Nevertheless, beginning in the 1850s, the rising meat prices that were being paid for "live" cattle brought about the advent of cattle drives. These drives, which began in Texas, would reach states like Missouri and Kansas.[3] In fact, one of the many feeder trails of the famous Chisholm Trail originated in the small Hidalgo County border town of Donna, Texas.[4] Cattle driving was briefly arrested because of the Civil War, but the trade was picked back up in the post–Civil War years. In fact, Edwin J. Foscue's study "Land Utilization in the Lower Rio Grande Valley of South Texas" points out, "Between 1866 and 1880, records show that 4,223,497 cattle were driven out of Texas for points in Kansas and Missouri," and additionally, "the Morgan Steamship Company contracted with the Spanish Government in Cuba for the shipment of Texas cattle to that island. After the 1865 monthly shipment of cattle from Texas, ports averaged from 1,200 to 1,500 head, the movement reaching its height about 1875 when more than 33,000 head of cattle were shipped to Cuba."[5] Foscue's research demonstrates that the cattle industry was a highly profitable trade for the ranchers of Texas, but like all businesses, it was susceptible to highs and lows, and it was the lows that contributed to the fall of the Mexican American in the Lower Rio Grande Valley.

The early days of ranching saw a well-entrenched Mexican American population in the Lower Rio Grande Valley. This was in large part since land in South Texas had long been passed on utilizing the old Spanish custom of landownership, which was continued during the Mexican control of the territory. In the Spanish colonial system, the land was passed down through families. These grants, referred to as *derechos* (rights), did not allow for subdividing of the land. The land was kept in possession by the family, not individual persons within the family.

The Lower Rio Grande Valley's adherence to the Spanish colonial system did not leave large amounts of land open to purchase by Anglo settlers. Consequently, those Anglos who did venture into the South Texas "frontier" had only one real option for pursuing any kind of wealth or economic enterprise, and that was to become part of Mexican American society. This could be done through a variety of methods, which included becoming *compadres* or *comadres* (literally "co-parent" but referring to a godmother or godfather). However, it was not only obtained in baptism but also as sponsors of a *quinceañera* (girl's fifteenth birthday celebration) or marriage. These delineations and connections to the family were held in high esteem by Spanish/Mexican families. Nonetheless, the one major method of gaining access to Mexican American society and possibly their land was through marriage.

In his book *Anglos and Mexicans in the Making of Texas, 1836–1986*, David Montejano describes the society of South Texas as one in which "in the post annexation politics of the area, ethnic divisions were secondary to those of class," referring to the fact that these unions and *compadrazgo* were kept within the social class each race belonged to. Historian Armando C. Alonzo points out that to Anglos, the landed Mexican elite were seen as being "equal citizens because they too had tamed the harsh grasslands of the region." However, this was a two-way road for Mexican Americans who also looked at the social status of the Anglos their daughters were marrying. Nonetheless, for whatever reason, these unions and social obligations created interdependence between the newly incoming Anglo populations and the Mexican American population of the Lower Rio Grande Valley. In time, this unique social interdependence of the two races would be changed by the economic changes that would come to the South Texas borderlands.

The end of large-scale ranching would have enormous consequences within South Texas, especially in the Lower Rio Grande Valley. The transition from ranching to farming would occur due to several factors. First, the cattle industry of South Texas, once it became connected to the larger cattle trails, was now susceptible to fluctuations in the national economy. Consequently, when the stock market experienced a drastic dip in 1885, the South Texas ranchers, especially the Mexican American ranchers, were hit hard by the drop in beef prices. Also, the once highly profitable trade with Cuba was undermined by the advent of both the railroad and the refrigerated car, which allowed for better-quality beef to be sold with the island nation. This set this region of the cattle industry on a downward spiral that reached its nadir by 1880. Also, the use of the railroad and the fencing of lands resulted in the infeasibility of cattle drives in general. One issue that plagued the Mexican American rancher

A South Texas farm. *Courtesy of the Weslaco Museum.*

was the fact that most of them were cash poor; their only real wealth was their ownership of land. Consequently, many Mexican American ranchers could not invest in improvements or new technologies that would have assisted their financial survival in lean times.

Additionally, the end of large-scale ranching in the South Texas borderlands was accompanied by the introduction of railroads. However, before they could be introduced into the Rio Grande Valley, the steamboat industry had to be dealt with, and its members included the growing Anglo ranching elite, mainly Richard King (owner of King Ranch) and Mifflin Kenedy. These men along with their ranch holdings were conducting a very profitable freight shipping business on their steamboats along the Rio Grande. The reason it was profitable was that there were no railroads in the Lower Rio Grande Valley, but residents who felt that their shipping prices were inflated hoped to bring the railroad down to the Valley. Nevertheless, these shrewd businessmen did their best to interfere with any hopes Valley residents had for a railroad. These men even went as far as bidding for the railroad contract, and when it was awarded to someone else, they managed to block construction because the nearest terminus at Brazos Santiago was on their land. (There is more on the history of the Rio Grande Valley railroad system in the next chapter.)

Of all the changes that came to the Lower Rio Grande Valley—such as various wars, like the Mexican War for Independence, Texas War for

Independence, Mexican-American War and Civil War—it would be the change from a predominantly ranching to an agricultural economy that would have the greatest consequence for the RGV. Its greatest impact was on the once amicable racial relations in the South Texas borderlands. The transition would expose just how important the "bridge populations" (intermarriage between Anglos and Mexican Americans) were to the cohesiveness of peaceful border life and how Mexican American landownership was indelibly linked to their social status among the Anglos, both longtime residents and those who came with Lower Rio Grande Valley agricultural boom, which would earn it the nickname the "Magic Valley." The need to exploit and profit from the newly built railroad that now connected to the rest of the United States was instrumental in transforming the dwindling ranching economy into agricultural fields. However, what was needed was for land speculators to market both the land and the South Texas borderlands as viable investments. The target for these new agricultural developments was the midwestern farmer. The first to begin transforming the South Texas ranchlands was Hidalgo County's John Shary. Geographers Christian Brannstrom and Matthew Newman's study of the creation of the Magic Valley, *Inventing the Magic Valley of South Texas, 1905–1941*, describes the inception:

> *The Magic Valley myth, beginning in the early 1900s in the pages of a railroad publication, included images that land developers reproduced and reworked into promotional materials. The place myth included place images that attempted to replace a contrary idea of the Lower Rio Grande Valley (LRGV) as lawless, and semiarid; in addition, boosters represented the natural environment as conducive to growing a wide range of crops year-round, with easily available irrigation and abundant labor* [the abundant labor being Mexicans and Mexican Americans].[6]

As part of this selling of the myth of the Magic Valley, tours were established to bring farmers down from the Midwest and encourage their investment and settlement in the lands of the Lower Rio Grande Valley. An article in the *Ireton Ledger* of Ireton, Iowa, on May 13, 1920, describes one such trip. The article's author describes his group's trip into the Magic Valley, including such details as making a stop at the farm of H.P. Hanson, where they "sampled some of the delicious fruits," and how "thirty-eight varieties of growing products" were being grown on Hanson's "40-acre farm." The author goes on to describe the marvels of the Magic Valley's

An image of the Magic Valley campaign published by Missouri Pacific Railroad. *Courtesy of the Museum of South Texas History, Mrs. I.C. Caswell Collection.*

irrigation system: "That which makes the valley a wonderland is climate, soil, and water, and the labor problem is a big item in which plenty of help can be secured at 1.50 per day."[7] Another article in the society section of the *Wellington Daily News* of Wellington, Kansas, boasts of the valley, "Forty acres in the Magic (Rio Grande Valley of Texas) will produce equal to or more than 160 acres in Kansas. We can prove by science why people live longer and have better health in the Magic Valley."[8] These descriptions reveal the type of propaganda at work, to not only pay for the investment in the railroad but also to capitalize on the enormous tracts of land that were becoming available due to the decline of the cattle industry.

The readily available cheap labor hinted at by the purveyors of the Magic Valley advertisements was, of course, the Mexican/Mexican American population of the South Texas borderlands. This labor was abundant due to two factors, the first being the decline of the cattle industry. This decline placed small and large *rancheros* (owners of ranches) in a financial crisis in which being cash poor led them to sell off their lands. This situation affected not only the *patrón* but the *peón* as well, for now, both groups found themselves homeless and unemployed. While some of the wealthier patrón were able to maintain either their lands or employment elsewhere, it was the small landowner and those he employed who now became cheap labor. Wage labor was a new and unstable element for the farmworker, because on the ranch under the patrón-peón system, one was employed year-round and was housed and provided for by the patrón. However, under the farm system, wages were earned only for the time it would take for the work to be done and as long as there were crops to plant or pick.[9]

In addition, the conversion from employment as a *vaquero* (cowboy/ranch hand) was seen as a demeaning societal downgrade. This was because the position and skill of the vaquero were prized by both the ranchero and the Anglo ranchers. Vaqueros saw farmwork as menial and below men of their skill, but with hard times came hard choices, and these once-proud vaqueros now found themselves employed in a profession that they once looked down on.[10] As a result, not only did the vaqueros find themselves in a lower social position, but they also had one group on whom they laid the blame, and that was the "foreign" Anglo farmer who came down from the Midwest to displace this once-proud segment of Mexican American society.

The influx of Anglo farmers from the north brought about a very different atmosphere in the Lower Rio Grande Valley. Mexican Americans began facing the same issues and treatment their brethren north of the Nueces and African Americans throughout the South had been experiencing—not being allowed in restaurants, movie houses, certain schools or parts of town. The racism of the North found its way via the Anglo newcomers to the valley.[11] The fact that there was no major opposition to the racist views of the incoming Anglos demonstrates just how essential the bridge population was to maintain at least a modicum of racial harmony. Sandos's investigation of the shift in demographics toward a more polarized society is evident in the sudden drop in the mixed-race population and the sudden increase in racism in the Lower Rio Grande Valley.

As a result of the major demographic changes in the Rio Grande Valley and the shifting racial views held by residents, there was an explosion of violence in the early 1900s that historians and local residents have referred to as *La Matanza*. Some of the targets were specifically Mexican American landowners as a method to acquire more lands for agricultural development. The phrase used at the time was that it was "easier to buy land from a widow." The result was more Mexican American farmworkers and fewer vaqueros.

CITY OF ALAMO

The city of Alamo, although established by Anglo settlers, holds ties with Spanish settlement and actually sits on three specific deeded lands: El Agostadero del Gato, granted to Maximo Dominguez in 1833; Santa Ana, granted to Benigno Leal in 1834; and Los Toritos, granted to Jose Trevino in 1834. All three portions of land came from Porcion 72 of Reynosa, which was intended to establish Mexican territory in the 1800s but was originally granted to Jose Maria Balli by the Spanish crown in 1787.[12] Porcion 72 was established by the Spanish to colonize and establish territory, an intent like Escandon's excursion through the Rio Grande. In the early twentieth century, these same land grants would become of even more importance, as the Alamo Tract would be filed in 1902 by P.E. Blalock and T.L. Hawkins, whose goal was to use this land as means for sugar production and cattle ranching.[13] In 1908, the two men established a railroad depot called Ebenezer, which later became Camp Ebenezer as settlers moved in, although this came to an end when both men sold the site to the Alamo Land and Sugar Company in 1909. The site underwent a name change to Swallow and then eventually Alamo, which still exists today.[14]

During the early twentieth century, much of the Rio Grande Valley was becoming an ideal location for cattle ranching and gradual agriculture, as the land was cheap and the weather was warm. Like the attractiveness of southern Texas and northern Mexico to the Spanish, Anglo settlers from the regions north of Texas would migrate into what was later labeled the Magic Valley, which, though arid, was spacious and summery year-round. Around the same time, the Lower Rio Grande Valley was becoming subdivided by various towns, such as Weslaco in 1919, Donna in 1911 and the city of Alamo's town progression. From 1902 to the 1920s, southern Texas in total was becoming an area of violence. Although the establishment of much of the Lower Rio Grande Valley, like that of the city of Alamo, was done in the primary years of the twentieth century, South Texas at large was experiencing a fever of racial and cultural tension during the latter years of the nineteenth century that would extend into the early twentieth century.

The valley towns we know today were being developed during a period of intense racism, and acts of violence stemmed from those racist sentiments.

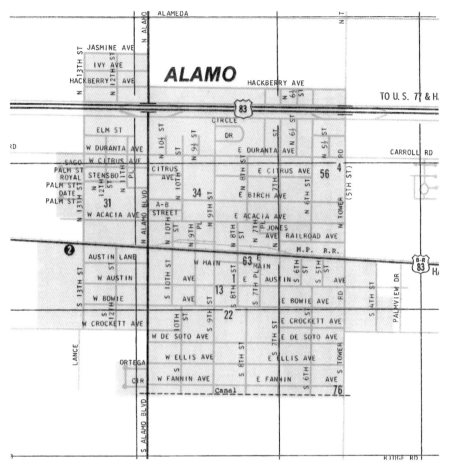

Map of the city of Alamo streets. *Courtesy of the City of Alamo Museum.*

This period of hate in South Texas left a legacy that would set the scene for the rest of the first half of the twentieth century in the RGV. For most Mexican families, education was not a guarantee, so manual or domestic labor was the only other option, but even at that, jobs such as farmwork or homemaking were dismissed in the professional realm, especially if it was a Mexican American worker. Stories of abuse and trauma in the work environment of farms are all too common, especially for those whose families worked the fields, such as the family of author Juan Carmona and numerous others. When considering the history of racism in South Texas, the question of why Mexican American workers were treated inhumanely is given a clearer answer.

THE ALAMO NEWS

ALAMO, HIDALGO COUNTY, TEXAS 78516, THURSDAY, JANUARY 3, 1974

Alamo's early days recounted from first newspaper edition

A LESS HAPPY TIME IN THE VALLEY— Unlike the 44th anniversary year of Alamo in 1967 when Hurricane Beulah left little to celebrate about, the Golden Anniversary of Alamo promises to be a time of much celebration. Hurricane damage photos of 1967 were taken by Lawrence E. Cron.

Alamo received name from cottonwood trees

(Written by C. H. Swallow at the request of the Alamo News Editor)

This community comes rightly by the usage of the name Alamo. There is never any thought on the part of those in authority of having any name for the town other than Alamo.

A part of the land making up the present Alamo Tract was a part of Portion 72 out of an officially unnamed tract known as the Alamo pasture, thus identified by the cottonwood trees along the river front. Alamo is the Spanish word for the cottonwood tree. Other parts of the tract were: Los Torritos Grant, known as the pasture of the little bulls, — a Spanish saint, — and part of the El Gato Grant, known as the pasture of the cat.

These divisions, all joining, were made pursuant to Mexican custom before there was a Republic or State of Texas. The purpose of those divisions was so that each owner had a segregated river frontage of his own to provide for domestic and stock water, and all use the whole area as a common stock range. These strips all run about 15 miles back from the river to the common north line of the original larger grants. As time went on ownership was changed by inheritance and sales and the area became known as the Alamo pasture.

These old titles were all confirmed in the original grantees, their heirs and assigns by the State of Texas after it became organized and a part of the U. S. A.

(Continued on Page 6)

Many changes seen in 50 years of time

NOTE — The people of Alamo are indebted to Perry Coler and the late Caroline Coler for preserving in permanent bound volume, the first newspaper ever published for this community, never other early local newspapers and every issue since they took over in March, 1928. Information for the following article was secured by Paul C. Netz from early editions of the Alamo News at the time of their 25th anniversary.

Practically every mode of life, except that of paying taxes, was entirely different back in 1918-19 when Alamo was in its infancy in comparison with the highly developed technical era we enjoy today. The first edition of "The Alamo News," dated August 7, 1918 carries a wealth of historical information concerning the pioneer era of this community.

The big headline, and, of course, the most important news at that time, read, "Swallow Starts New Land Company Now." The sub-caption says "Will Open Up Fine New Tract East of Alamo, Near Donna Irrigation Plant." Delving into the text, we read as follows:

"A deal that was to be expected now that practically all the Alamo Tract has been sold to individual farmers, is the entrance of C. H. Swallow & Company into the colonization business in the Valley.

"This company is organized by Mr. R. B. Creager, of Brownsville, Texas, president of the Alamo Land & Sugar Co., and C. H. Swallow of Lincoln,

Nebraska, general manager of the Alamo Land & Sugar Co.

"They have purchased practically all the brush land in the Donna irrigation district north of the railroad, amounting to about 9,000 acres, which was formerly owned by the Beamer Syndicate.

"The Alamo Land & Sugar Company and C. H. Swallow & Company will operate together until the remaining lands of the Alamo company are sold. There is no change in the officers, directors, or management of the Alamo Company. The Alamo Company business will be continued until their lands which comprise a total of about 38,000 acres, are all sold.

The remainder of the article went on to name the sales force and to describe the various features of the new land, mentioning "A most recent addition to the district canal system is the installation of two 48-inch pumps."

Taxes Not New 1918

Taxes were not new in 1918 but luxury tax ... not as high as now. Just ... foregoing article on the front page a caption reads, "Ten Per Cent Luxury Tax Causes No Alarm Here." "The new tax on luxuries isn't troubling Alamo farmers very much so far as can be learned. The people who are buying automobiles, piano players, graphophones, sporting goods, cameras and similar articles that will be taxed under the new Federal law are going to 'Come across' cheerfully as long as needed. They want the good things of life, and a matter

(Continued on Page 2)

Alamo News 1974 edition recalling the history of the city of Alamo. *Courtesy of the City of Alamo Museum.*

The original postmark for the city of Alamo under its previous name, Forum. *Courtesy of the City of Alamo Museum.*

Despite the saddening legacy, there is still room to acknowledge and commemorate the early families of the RGV, as well as the culture and demographic that have grown from those origins. Although they were faced with extreme prejudice, many early families in the city of Alamo went on to hold prominence in the community through business initiatives and cultural unity. Acacia Street, for example, was known as the "Main Street for Mexican families."[15] In retrospect, Acacia Street provided an environment in which the Mexican American community felt most comfortable shopping and becoming business owners. Most frequently, farmers and ranchers would utilize Acacia Street to supply their workers with grocery runs on the weekends.[16] A day on Acacia Street would consist of the women buying groceries for the week, the men visiting the barbershop or *cantinas* and, when possible, family time at a restaurant or at the movie theater to watch Mexican movies.[17] Environments facilitated by places like Acacia Street allowed for Mexican American culture to continue to flourish and survive in Alamo and the Rio Grande Valley at large.

An interesting pattern found in the accounts of Alamo natives is that almost all hold experiences of working in the fields as farmworkers, even as young schoolchildren or business owners. The Contreras family, for example, while being business owners on the infamous Acacia Street, had to leave for half of the year to make their journey up north for migrant farmwork, and the other half of the year was spent working in their family business as well as Alamo packing sheds.[18] Like in most migrant farmworker families, most Mexican American children who worked on farms would not receive a full or equal education due to their six-month absence from school. Alamo native, veteran and educator Rafael Garza, born on Acacia Street, served in the U.S. Army, but his childhood consisted of school, along with farmwork after school, on the weekends and through the migratory months in summer and fall.[19] Similarly, Alonso and Noe Garza, Alamo natives and Alamo police officers, went to school as young children but also had to work after school and on the weekends.[20] Rodolfo Villarreal, an Alamo native as well as a veteran, recalls attending what was known as the "Mexican School" during school days and working at his parents' store on Acacia Street after school and on the weekends.[21] The Mexican American community, whether by farm working, business initiatives, military, police or even educational career paths, served the Alamo community wholeheartedly, from childhood to adulthood.

When looking into the history of the city of Alamo, there is one other significant event to the community, and that is an infamous bank robbery that occurred in the city. On April 22, 1961, the First State Bank in Alamo was robbed. The story goes that a certain J.M. Bobo (fifty-three) from Fort Worth, Texas, broke into the bank via the roof by cutting through it in the early morning hours before any employee came into the building. He was wearing a homemade cloth hood to cover his face, with only some eye holes cut out so that he could see and function. He sat inside and waited for the first employees to make their way into the building. He had a small revolver in his possession and encountered the bank's janitor first, Manuel Cortez, age sixty-seven. Next was the bank's vice president, W.S. Ray, followed by some bank tellers. Once Bobo got everyone secured by tying their ankles and wrists with some cord, he forced Ray to open the vault. Inside the vault, he was able to collect $35,000, which was in dominations of $1 to $20 bills, all of which he stuffed into a laundry bag he had with him for that very purpose. He then made his way to the back door and out into the alley.

A business on Alamo's Acacia Street. *Courtesy of the City of Alamo Museum.*

Barrera Radio Service Shop, a local business in Alamo. The owner was the taxi driver who picked up the robber of the Alamo bank. *Courtesy of the City of Alamo Museum.*

Inside, cashier Evelyn Morin was able to free herself and then Ray, who promptly called the police to report the robbery. He described the robber "as polite and soft-spoken. He was neatly dressed in khaki pants and a short-sleeved khaki shirt. He wore a brown short-brimmed hat over the hood." Amazingly, Bobo apparently did not have a fluid escape plan and walked over to a nearby service station, sack in hand, to a pay phone located at the station and called for a taxi. Aurelio Barrera arrived and dropped Bobo off on Main Street in Donna, Texas. From there, Bobo called another taxi to take him to his hotel, which lay between the nearby cities of Donna and Weslaco. After he dropped off Bobo, Barrera then went to pick up some car parts in the city of San Juan. It was not until he got back to Alamo that he learned about the bank robbery and quickly made the connection to the passenger he had picked up in the area of the bank who was carrying a full laundry sack. By this point, law enforcement had set up roadblocks on all roads leading out of the valley, especially toward Mexico.

An image from the *Alamo News* of the arrest of "The Alamo Bank Robbery" suspect J.M. Bobo. *Courtesy of the City of Alamo Museum.*

The First State Bank of Alamo, which was the subject of a robbery in 1961. *Courtesy of the City of Alamo Museum.*

Barrera informed authorities about his passenger, and that sent them down the path of tracking him down at his hotel. All they needed to know was where Barrera had dropped him off, and they were able to find the taxi that had picked him up and taken him to his hotel. There they gave the description to the hotel manager, and they were able to locate which room he was staying in. They surrounded the area with state and local authorities while Sheriff's Deputies Heriberto Sanchez and R.G. Perez and State Highway Patrolman Sergeant S.M. Moxely made their way into Bobo's room. They came into the room just as the suspect was walking out of the shower. They identified themselves and made their way through the door. They asked for the gun that he had used in the bank robbery; he handed it over to them, and they found most of the $35,000 in a suitcase and placed him under arrest. Afterward, it would come to light that he had been in town for several days planning his robbery and had been seen around town by residents days before the crime.[22]

RGV TRAIN HISTORY

In our lived experiences, railroads have symbolized many things, both positive and negative. Railroads usually have positive connotations of acting as a connection between urban and rural, but by discussing this in-depth, we have concluded that the history of industrialization has not always been beneficial to our community and to people of color. The way that we view railroads is starkly different from the general observation. In the Rio Grande Valley, and in many other places, a railroad symbolizes the segregation between the "good" and "bad" sides of town, and unfortunately, this meant that people were divided by class and deliberately segregated by race. Living on one side of the tracks could determine your standard of life, the school you would attend and whether or not you had access to libraries, recreation centers or well-made infrastructure. Additionally, a railroad meant the stealing of land for many, because as industrialization progressed, colonial dominance overtook our native lands, as well as the cultural and physical ties we had to it. Similarly, the construction of a railroad meant quite literally cutting through land that had natural elements and biodiversity that peoples were culturally and historically connected to. Labor was exploited, and many suffered in the creation of railroads for the sake of industrialization. In this story, a railroad means the difference between prosperity or misfortune and life or death.

The first railway built south of the Houston–San Antonio area was from Corpus Christi to Laredo. It started out as the Corpus Christi, San Diego and Rio Grande Railroad, a narrow-gauge railroad that was built in the

Map of the Missouri Pacific lines in South Texas. *Courtesy of Museum of South Texas History, Mrs. I.C. Caswell Collection.*

late 1870s. "Narrow gauge" refers to the distance between the inside of one track on the line and the inside of its parallel track. In a standard railway, the distance is 1,435 millimeters, but in a narrow gauge, it is 762 or 610 millimeters. There are several reasons for these different types of tracks; one is that curves can be made much tighter in places of difficult terrain like hills, mountains and forests. This also saves money in a variety of ways, such as not having to make tunnels as wide and with less steel for the lighter rails that are used. The drawback is that the train cannot travel as fast or carry as much cargo as a train on a standard rail.[23]

The man in charge of building the Corpus Christi, San Diego and Rio Grande Railroad was Uriah Lott, a businessman out of Albany, New York, who, upon his arrival in South Texas, engaged in the shipping industry in the coastal city of Corpus Christi. He chartered ships to take wool to New York and earned a position on the board of the Corpus Navigation Company. All the while, he had a genuine interest in the railroad industry. This led him to join the efforts of Richard King and Mifflin Kennedy to bring a railroad into the Rio Grande Valley. The road to the final completion was a long one, taking over seven years, and with a delay this long, it came to be known as "Lott's Folly." Although Lott's name is the one that is most often associated with the building of what would become known as the "Spiderweb Railroad" in South Texas, it was another man who really made it come to fruition.[24]

Benjamin Yoakum came into the picture as an employee of Lott. His previous work experience was as a passenger agent for the International and Great Northern Railroad, and his chief job was recruiting immigrants from Europe to settle in areas along railroad lines. In the early twentieth century, there was a large wave of immigrants from eastern Europe, often called "new immigrants" by the older western European immigrants. They often arrived through Ellis Island and made their way to the already overcrowded cities, which were bursting at the seams. Lack of housing and infrastructure made finding another place to settle and seek out their American dream very attractive, but where in this strange land? This is where people like Yoakum stepped in to try to find them a place to settle and at the same time support the railroads by providing businesses and employees to serve those who were riding the rails. Consequently, Benjamin Yoakum learned the ins and outs of running railroads, which is why Lott hired him to be his chief clerk for the San Antonio and Aransas Pass Railroad.

In time, Yoakum was leading three major rail lines: the St. Louis and San Francisco Railroad (known locally as the Frisco), the Rock Island Railroad and the Gulf Coast Lines. It was his acquisition of the Gulf Coast Lines that allowed him to shift control of South Texas's rails from the Southern Pacific to his Gulf Coast Lines, a move that put him in control of the area's railroad development. He also wanted to create a series of connections that would take passengers from Memphis to Mexico City via the cities of New Orleans, Houston and Brownsville. Sadly, this grand idea came to an end when his Frisco lines went into bankruptcy.

Nonetheless, throughout his machinations over the years, he was convinced that South Texas was ripe for development. He earnestly believed that if he could connect the Rio Grande Valley to major national markets, it would become attractive to a plethora of business interests and there would be a boom in real estate and other related industries, especially in the agricultural business. He schemed long and hard to see his dream realized, even getting the State of Texas to allow for the consolidation of six small rail companies, including the Red River Texas and Southern Railroad Company. This move brought him more control of rail lines in Texas, but it was not simple ownership of rail lines that he would need to fulfill his plans; it was the fact that any attempt at connecting the Rio Grande Valley to a larger rail network would require the tracks to run through the land of the King Ranch (the largest ranch in Texas, encompassing most of South Texas).

He began a vigorous correspondence with Robert Kleberg to generate the interest of key landowners of South Texas in his plan to develop the railway into the Valley. A crucial meeting occurred in St. Louis in 1902 between Yoakum and several potential investors, which resulted in the St. Louis Trust Company offering up a grand total of $800,000 in bonds. This was coupled with an agreement that landowners—the Kings, Klebergs, Armstrongs and Yturrias—would donate lands to form land companies to create towns along the future rail lines. Furthermore, the investors requested that land within four miles of the city of Brownsville, an additional sixty acres within the city, be donated to their efforts to set up a depot and potential shops that would service passengers on the railroad.

Kleberg led the creation of the company that would begin to survey the potential lands for the railway. Yoakum suggested his former boss Lott as president of the company and the one to lead the construction of the rail system. Joining Lott would be Kleberg as vice president and Mifflin Kenedy as secretary. Other notable investors in the corporations were names like Sam Fordyce, Francisco Yturria, Robert Driscoll Sr. and Jr. and J.B. Armstrong. Some of these same investors would lead the formation of the American Land and Irrigation Company in 1905, which would support the irrigation efforts in the Valley, a technology needed to transform the RGV's ranch land into a land ripe for farming. An offshoot of that company with the same investors was the Capisallo Land and Development Company, which purchased land to establish the town of Mercedes, a name chosen to honor Mexican president Porfirio Díaz's wife. These investors were courting the Mexican president in order to earn his cooperation in connecting rail lines into Mexico. These men would also work under the direction of South Texas political boss Jim Wells, who assisted with the acquisition of land and titles.

Seeing his plans finally coming to fruition, Yoakum began to purchase large amounts of land, including 39,000 acres in Hidalgo County. Yoakum—along with Thomas Carter, a grain merchant and part of the St. Louis Railroad Syndicate—chartered the American Rio Grande Land and Irrigation Company. These two men, under their chartered company, amassed over 104,000 acres of land and became the most successful irrigation company in the Rio Grande Valley. Johnston Brothers Construction out of Illinois earned the contract to lay the rails south to the Rio Grande Valley. It, in turn, subcontracted the laying of the tracks to Sam Robertson's Contracting Company. Construction was faced with a variety of obstacles, including financial issues, the contraction of yellow fever by the workers, lack of materials and just plain inexperience with a project this large. Nonetheless, on July 4, 1904, there was more than the nation's Independence Day to celebrate. On that day, the very first locomotive made its way into the border city of Brownsville.

The construction and existence of these newly built rail lines led to the establishment of several towns along its path such as Robstown, Bishop, Sarita, Raymondville, Lyford, Sebastian, Harlingen, San Benito and Olmito. Shortly after the first train made its way into Brownsville, Yoakum was thanked via telegram "for giving us our independence by the completion of the Lott Road, which connects us with the outside world. In honor of the advent of the railroad, the citizens' Council will tomorrow change Brownsville's time from sun to standard." This statement was about the fact that since Brownsville was now connected to national and international markets, it would have to conform to standard time to facilitate business with the outside world. Although the investors imagined a multitude of rail connections south into Mexico, the collapse of the Díaz regime during the Mexican Revolution ended those hopes. But the initial connection through Brownsville would enable international shipping of goods in and out of Mexico. As a result of the completion of a railroad into the Rio Grande Valley, agribusiness would boom, along with land acquisition as real estate in South Texas became more and more lucrative.[25]

TRAIN OPERATIONS

To understand how the accident played out, it is important to have a basic understanding of how trains operated at the time of the accident in 1940. According to the Interstate Commerce Commission (ICC) report, the train in use at the time of the accident was a Missouri Pacific IVN Engine 351. The train itself consisted of six cars: "two baggage cars, one baggage-express car, one coach, and one Pullman sleeping car, in the order named; all cars were of steel construction," and the engine would be in the lead.[26] This type of train would have the following employees operating the train, each with their own set of duties: the fireman, the conductor, the brakeman, the engineer and the Pullman Porter. Two of these four positions, the engineer and the fireman, worked in tandem. These are two of the most highly trained and technical positions in the railroad industry. The engineer is tasked with overseeing and controlling a steam boiler and overall control of the speed of the train. He also oversees all the gauges, speed, temperature and brake line pressure. Most engineers are specific to certain areas of the line since they need to know the terrain well to anticipate what would be needed on that particular journey such as inclines, declines and turns. All of this requires them to think ahead in order to maintain a proper speed and control of the train itself. This is much like the men who captain a ship on the Mississippi; each one knows his own piece of that enormous river that winds, dips and has all types of debris. Each one comes to know that part of the river, and he therefore takes over the navigation of any boat coming through his particular area. Engineers need to know by heart the

Weslaco Railroad Depot, circa 1920. *Courtesy of the Weslaco Museum.*

terrain they will encounter and when to increase or decrease speed to safely maneuver the train through their section of track. This is why they work directly with the fireman.

A fireman's job is literally to control the fire, which increases the temperature of the boiler and then adds power to the engines. This is done not just by randomly shoveling coal into the fire, as seen in many movies, but by carefully spreading it out evenly in the firebox so that heat is distributed throughout the box. This provides for a more controlled temperature. The fireman works in tandem with the engineer because, to speed up or slow down, he needs to know how much fire to add to the firebox. These are both highly technical skills that require specialized training. When it comes to the train that was running on the day of the accident, they may have been using oil and not coal. The concept was the same; the oil came in through a pump and had to spray evenly into the firebox to also have a controlled temperature.[27] Additionally on board that day was the brakeman. The brakeman's job was to control the braking system. This involved him running on the roof from car to car turning the brake wheels on each of the cars to fully stop the train.[28] However, when it comes to the overall person in charge, the captain of the ship, that would be the conductor. The role of the conductor evolved from the position of ship's captain, someone who oversaw everything and everyone. Indeed, his role was far beyond taking tickets; he was the one who gave the go-ahead proclaiming it safe to take off and would take over the train whenever an emergency occurred, such as an accident.[29]

One thing that is always on the mind of the conductor is time. All trains have to attempt to be on time and keep up with their assigned schedule, a task that is daunting in the least. Issues constantly arise that have the conductor adjusting. Professor James Porterfield explains it as such:

The train is running on a schedule. Locomotive engineers and train conductors have a timetable. It's the same general principle, but the timetable is broken down into minutes and perhaps even partial minutes as to how long you must get from point A to point B and how long from point B to Point C. That's how they control the movement of the train, especially back in those pre–World War Two days, when everything was really done by hand. They didn't have computers or any type of telecommunications equipment, all they had were telegraphs and signal systems that controlled the movement of the trains. So, a train would have a schedule to run from point A to point B, and it was supposed to be at Point B in 15 minutes and 30 seconds after they left the station. Then they had another 18 minutes to get to Point C and then they had 12 minutes to get to Point B and they knew that. Now if something happened in the meantime like an oncoming train had to change its schedule, then the dispatcher (that's the person that's controlling the movement of the trains) he's sitting at a yard office. He would send a telegraph to the station that was somewhere between those two trains and notify that station agent, to stop the northbound train at Station C and have it take a siding so that the southbound train can go through on the mainline track. This gets their schedule changed, so all that complicated stuff is going on as they're trying to move the trains from these different points. The other thing we're talking about is a passenger train. So, whatever its schedule was, the locomotive engineer was trying to keep to his schedule. That would determine the speed that he was going.[30]

This would all come into play to affect how fast or slow a train is going at a particular time. There is never any real constant speed as they are always running.

Another position of note was the porter, sometimes called Pullman Porters since they worked within the Pullman cars, serving as attendants to the passengers. In the post–Civil War era, train travel began to see its height of prestige and accessibility, especially with the completion of the Transcontinental Railroad. This late 1800s period would see the use of Pullman sleeping cars, which would have Pullman Porters attending them, most of whom were African American. Many of these men were formerly enslaved peoples, and although this was a position of servitude, the job of porter was seen by African Americans as highly coveted. This was not a continuation of slavery like sharecropping; you worked indoors, and unlike most African Americans, you could travel and see parts of the country you otherwise would not see. Not to mention that the job provided a steady income. Nonetheless, porters did experience long hours and low pay compared to other workers on the train. They eventually formed a union called the Brotherhood of Sleeping Car Porters, which, after a twelve-year fight, managed to improve pay and working conditions. Their experiences in the long strike gave them the tools that would later be employed in the struggle for civil rights, in which they would also contribute some of this new pay to the cause.[31]

This brief overview of the functions and operations of a train in 1940 provides an understanding of what was going on inside the train as it approached the intersection of Tower Road and Highway 83. Just like what happened in the truck driven by Mr. Ramon, there are many variables that could have affected the events of that tragic day. However, understanding the operations inside the train does help paint a part of the whole scene of that day. The more voices and understanding we can provide will help fill in the gaps of the unknown and hopefully provide some clarity to the events of that day.

THE LIVES OF FARMWORKERS

The authors of this book grew up as children of farmworkers, which is one of the reasons that this project is near and dear to our hearts. I (Juan) grew up hearing stories of life as a migrant farmworker, and one thing that really stayed in my consciousness is that at times my grandparents, parents, aunts and uncles would be housed in old chicken coops. This really made me think of how my family was viewed by their employers. This idea that a chicken coop was good enough for them struck me as degrading and dehumanizing. These were my loved ones, the most caring, hardworking people I knew, and that hurt deep down as I grew up. This was coupled with my father always feeling uneasy around white people, telling me that he remembered the nasty and derogatory names and comments they would make toward his sisters. So deep down, I always looked at farmwork as a negative experience. However, I also heard my family laugh at some of their experiences, telling funny stories, and I came to see it as a bonding experience as well.

The farmworkers in this story were not working as migrant farmworkers at the time of the crash, but like our families, they went where the work took them, which was at times to local fields. As discussed in a previous chapter, in the early twentieth century, the Valley's demographics, landscape and economy had undergone an enormous shift into the agricultural industry, and by 1940, agribusiness was well underway. The cities in the Rio Grande Valley not only had fields of crops but also hosted myriad packing and processing sheds to prepare the crops for local and national markets.

Agricultural workers. *Courtesy of the Weslaco Museum.*

There was plenty of work to be had for families to engage in and support themselves.

The nature of the environment and the soil allowed for a wide variety of crops to be grown in the South Texas border region. One crop that was synonymous with the South was cotton. Even to this day, cotton is grown in the Valley. The picking of cotton is backbreaking labor, sometimes referred to as stoop labor, for workers spend their time stooped over since cotton plants do not grow taller than three feet high. Workers would have to reach down and twist the fluffy lint from the bulb, but they had to be careful because the boll had sharp ends and could easily cut them, which presented its own problems. If you cut yourself, the cotton that was stained with blood was worth nothing, even if you had filled numerous sacks of cotton. Once you were done filling a basket or a sack with the product, you would have to get in line to await a chip. This type of currency was the way a farmworker would be paid; a specific number of chips totaled how much you would be paid in actual money. You had to keep these chips to be paid later, which made them very valuable to the workers, so they held onto them with a watchful eye.

Another crop that is prevalent in the Rio Grande Valley is sugar cane. As Valley residents, we all know about sugarcane because the process of burning the cane sends ashes throughout the Valley, and as children, we

A Rio Grande Valley farmworker. *Courtesy of the Weslaco Museum.*

often dirtied our hands and ourselves playing with the ash as it descended on us, angering many a mother. The cane is burned to reduce the number of leaves, stalks and anything else that needs to be removed prior to collecting the cane. During the present day, because people may be in the fields before the burn, a system of loud sirens blows to warn people that the burning is going to commence. Before the use of machines, once the cane was burned, it had to be hand cut, which was dangerous and backbreaking work.

Citrus—from oranges to the famous Ruby Red Grapefruit—was an agricultural product that early on became one of the most successful crops for the Rio Grande Valley. These were picked by workers on ladders who would have a *costale* or sack over their shoulders, in which they placed the fruit once they had twisted it off the stem. These costales were used in the harvesting of other plants that were grown in South Texas. Crops like strawberries, onions, carrots and tomatoes were picked by farmworkers, and all utilized these sacks to place their items in. Once the sack was full, it was taken to either the truck or another designated area and unloaded.

When these costales were being unloaded, either the *mayordomo* (crew leader) or a member of his family would keep track of how much was being picked by a particular individual. He would have a notebook with the names of the workers, and he would place a mark next to each person's name to keep track of how much they picked. Often, it was tracked not

39

A tractor hauling sugarcane in Pharr, Texas. *Courtesy of the Weslaco Museum.*

just by an individual but as a family with children. The adults or older teens may have their names on the book, but the younger ones were often placed under their fathers' names. Depending on the method that was negotiated for pay for the workers, there were times when one was paid an hourly wage, but the most advantageous method that garnered more pay was by how much an individual or family would pick. Hence, the use of wood chips or marks on a notebook. Additionally, depending on how the contracts were negotiated, families could be assigned a whole row or rows to pick of a particular crop.

For those who were not too exhausted, the ten- to twelve-hour workday (sunup to sundown) did not end with emptying their sacks; they would go on to work in the packing sheds, where they would continue to work at an hourly wage, sorting the fruit and removing the bad fruit from what had been picked that day. Not all participated in this part of the workday. Usually it was those who were younger and had more energy to keep working after putting in most of their time under the hot sun. However, this was another method to supplement their income, so many families and individuals continued working into the night.

For farmworkers in the fields of South Texas (in 1940 they used the phrase "fruit picker"), a typical day would begin with the mother or grandmother waking up around 5:00 a.m. to make breakfast and lunch for the family. They would fill containers with water to make it through the hot days; in

Left: A grapefruit packing shed. *Courtesy of the Weslaco Museum.*

Below: A grapefruit canning plant in Weslaco, Texas. *Courtesy of the Weslaco Museum.*

the RGV, temperatures could easily exceed one hundred degrees. By 6:00 a.m., the family was up, having their breakfast and coffee as they awaited the mayordormo to make his way over to their house to transport them to the field they would be working in that day.

Mayordormos used large trucks with big beds, such as the one that was involved in the accident at Alamo. These trucks served a variety of purposes and were a major investment for the crew chief. The bed of the truck would usually have what the workers would refer to in Spanish as *redillas* (boards that ran along the sides of the truck to keep the passengers secured in the

Farmworkers in South Texas. *Courtesy of Taylor Seaver.*

back), as well as a tarp that would go over the top to keep the elements out and provide some shade on a hot day. These boards would also be utilized if the truck was transporting the fruit to the packing sheds. These redillas could also be easily removed and the truck could be used as a flatbed to transport supplies and equipment.

The workers would wait for the truck to pull up and honk for the workers to come out and board for the workday. Sometimes, for whatever reason, one would step out and say to the crew chief, "Ahora no voy" ("I am not coming in today"). This was a phrase that workers would use as a joke among themselves when they were working to either make fun of someone who had not come or to express that they wished they could skip a day of work and just stay home and relax. For all the struggle these families went through, there was a sense of camaraderie that developed among the workers who were drawn together through the harsh work and conditions. They would tell each other stories as they worked, sing songs, tell jokes, anything to pass the time.

When it comes to the environment that they did work in, there were obvious dangers and hidden dangers. While working in the fields, there was always the danger of being bitten by insects, which could lead to an infection and inability to work. There would also be the occasional snake that would be found as they were pulling vegetables from the ground or even under the shade of the trucks. There was also the hidden danger of what was all around them. In the 1940s, pesticides were still in their infancy, only recently being introduced in the 1930s, and their dangers were not readily known. Their abundant use would lead to cancers and other diseases. Not to mention the fact that the labor itself would leave its marks on the bodies of the workers through back problems, swollen fingers, cuts, bruises and dehydration.

For families with children, there was also an impact on their schooling and, for some young girls, added responsibilities. Families who had babies and toddlers would have limited options when it came to childcare. They could sometimes keep the little ones alongside them, but one other common option was to engage an older sister (usually a young teen) as a babysitter who watched her younger siblings and young children from other families that did not have someone to leave them with. They would all be at the field where the family was working but usually off to the side, perhaps near vehicles so that they were not in the way of the workers. When it came to education, there was a variety of ways that children could attend school. They could go to school on off seasons or even work on the weekends to help supplement their family's income. Sadly, the shorter school year and work in general would have a negative impact on some students' education, not to mention that sometimes dropping out became a choice if the family was struggling due to a loss or injury of a family member.

According to interviews after the Alamo train crash, there were quite a few teenage girls on the truck that day. Most of these girls were from Starr County, mostly from La Rosita. Small towns like La Rosita had a limited population of potential suitors. This was a problem in an era when opportunities were limited to women in general, let alone women of Mexican descent. For some families, the best they could do for their young women was to offer a suitable marriage to someone who could provide for them when they came of marrying age.

In the conservative Mexican American society of South Texas, the social life of young women or teenage girls was strictly regulated, with most of their social life centered on family celebrations or community events. A young lady's presence was always accompanied by a chaperone of some sort, either a brother, cousin, uncle or another trusted individual. Scholar Vicki Ruiz describes this system as chaperonage and states that it "is best understood

Farmworkers in South Texas. *Courtesy of Taylor Seaver.*

as a manifestation of familial oligarchy whereby elders attempted to dictate the activities of the youth for the sake of family honor."[32] These social interactions and chaperonage were then extended to working in the fields, for some of these women were sent to work in the more populous Mid-Valley area (where Alamo was located) to meet potential suitors. This was a very regulated environment with a chaperone to keep a watchful eye on the ladies' and families' honor. Tragically, this was why so many young women were on Ramon's work crew that day.

This was the daily life of those who boarded Jose Ramon's truck that fateful morning. They were just people working to support themselves and their families via the type of work that was available to them—work that is still being done to this day, in the same fields, traveling down the same roads and living in the same neighborhoods. As we move forward toward the events of that tragic day, keep in mind that before the horror, there were lives being lived, laughter and love. All of this is still remembered today by those who were left behind.

PART II

THE COLLISION

RAMON FAMILY HISTORY

Northern Mexico and South Texas were not always separated into fragments. Once, this land was home to Spanish colonists, Indigenous peoples and many other European immigrants. Because of the cultural mixture that marked the climate of the Valley, RGV natives are able to trace their ancestry to the South Texas borderlands, with family trees rooted long before national borders were placed. The Ramon family can trace their roots back to the state of Tamaulipas, specifically to the city of Mier, also called El Paso del Cántaro. The family left that area around 1871 to move into La Rosita in Starr County.[33] It was during their residence in Starr County that the Ramon family began to grow, with Cesario and Ruperta, parents of Jose Ramon, beginning their family on a small ranch. Eventually, monetary needs exceeded what their ranch could produce, and the family decided to move north to the town of Runge.[34] It was not until 1930 that the Ramon family moved to the small town of Garceno in Starr County, ten years before the Alamo train crash of 1940 claimed the lives of Jose Ramon, the youngest of the Ramon family, and his two sons Leonel and Raul.[35]

The move back to Starr County meant more economic opportunities, as the Lower Rio Grande Valley during the 1930s and 1940s was transforming itself from a ranching region to that of an agricultural-based economy. This economic transformation meant an increase in jobs for those in the agricultural sector of work, especially for those who organized crews of workers and negotiated with the farmers. This newfound system created the role that Jose Ramon would eventually fill and use to provide for his family

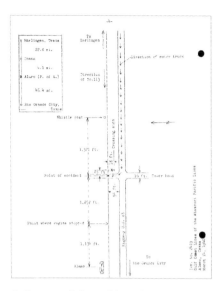

A diagram of the accident. *Courtesy of Interstate Commerce Commission Report 1940.*

of twelve: the job of the mayordormo (crew leader). The role of the mayordormo was found throughout the agricultural industry, and it held the most responsibility; mayordormos had the task of ensuring that the ranch or farm owner would have a crew scheduled to pick when needed, as well as securing all crew members, providing transportation, picking a designated field to work and planning a solid route. He negotiated the wages for his workers and at times distributed them himself. The wage was based on the amount to be picked, the time and the number of workers needed for the job. Jose Ramon was not only a career agricultural worker, *troquero* (truck driver/owner) and mayordormo, but he was also the father and main provider of eleven children and his wife, Natividad. Jose epitomized entrepreneurship, using his recently bought work truck to take himself and his crew of forty or more workers to their fields, as well as serving as the middleman between farmworker and farm owner.

When it came to recruiting workers, Ramon would do his best to provide opportunities for members of his community in Starr County, specifically La Rosita, where he knew many families who needed work. He would drive over to their homes and bring those who wanted to work back to his home in Donna, where they could stay for the duration of the job. Consequently, many who were lost on that fateful day were from Starr County, and you can find many buried together in the town of Escobares.

In 1940, Highway 83 (or Business 83) was the route that would connect those from the Lower Rio Grande Valley to the agricultural fields usually found on the outskirts of towns. Highway 83 was also the route that Jose Ramon frequented on those early mornings when there was work to do, meeting and picking up his crew for the long day ahead. The daily life of an agricultural worker was a routine: waking early, preparing the mind and body for a grueling day in the elements and then boarding the mayordormo's work truck to travel to the field. It was on the intersection of Highway 83 and Tower Road that Jose Ramon, his two sons and his group of workers

MISSION DISTRICT—BETWEEN HARLINGEN AND RIO GRANDE CITY

Station Numbers	Distance from Harlingen	TIME TABLE No. 22 — Taking Effect JULY 23, 1939 — STATIONS	Siding Capacity in Cars	FIRST CLASS 113 Local Passenger Daily	SECOND CLASS 561 Red Ball Freight Daily	125 Mixed Daily Except Sunday	THIRD CLASS 597 Local Freight Daily Except Sunday
25	0.0	CS........HARLINGEN.....OWYS	Yard	L 7.10 AM	L 6.45 AM		L 7.45 AM
A4	4.3	STUART PLACE	98	7.20	7.00		8.00
A6	6.2	ADAMS GARDENS	14	7.23			8.05
A8	8.3	D........LA FERIA	155	s 7.27	7.15		9.00
14	13.9	D........MERCEDES........W	139	s 7.40 561	7.40 113		9.50
19	18.8	D........WESLACO........Y	75	s 7.50	8.00		10.30
23	22.8	D........DONNA	113	s 8.00	8.15		11.10 596
27	26.9	D........ALAMO	86	s 8.08	8.25		11.35
29	29.3	D........SAN JUAN........Y	98	s 8.14	8.35		11.55 AM
31	31.0	D........PHARR	93	s 8.19	8.45		12.30 PM
34	34.2	D........McALLEN	112	s 8.29	9.05 596		1.20
	34.3	T.& N.O. CROSSING					
40	40.0	D........MISSION........OWYS	Yard	A 8.45 AM 596	A 9.30 AM	L 10.45 AM	A 1.45 PM
42	41.7	MAMIE				10.52	
45	45.5	CHIHUAHUA				f 11.03	
55	53.3	P........SAM FORDYCE	47			s 11.25	
56	56.4	P........CURVITAS				s 11.35	
60	59.8	RATCLIFF	16			s 11.55	
61	60.7	LA GRULLA				f 11.58 AM	
65	65.3	GARCIAS	12			f 12.10 PM	
73	73.3	D........RIO GRANDE CITY........Y	Yard			A 12.40 PM	
				Daily	Daily	Daily Except Sunday	Daily Except Sunday

78.8

KINGSVILLE DIVISION

The Rio Grande Valley train schedule. *Courtesy of the City of Alamo Museum.*

would find themselves surrounded by the mist and chill of the early morning of March 14, 1940, sheltered only by the walls of the truck and the tarpaulin covering. Eventually, they possibly stalled on the railroad tracks and met Gulf Coast Lines Engine Number 351, Train Number 113.

THE CRASH

In the early morning of March 14, 1940, dew and mist coated the Valley while Jose Ramon and two of his sons, Leonel and Raul, prepared themselves and Jose's newly purchased work truck to transport approximately forty-two workers to a citrus grove in Edinburg, Texas. According to Israel Ramon Jr., grandson of Jose Ramon, Jose was a very strict father who wanted all his sons to be clean-cut and have short hair. That morning, he saw Israel, his oldest son, with hair that was already touching his ears and told him he could not join them that day to work. Israel cried because he really wanted to go and be with his brothers (they were very close), but he had to stay behind.[36] Whether by destiny or chance, this action saved Israel's life and allowed for his descendants to be alive now and act as participants in this research.

The night before, the work truck had been broken into, resulting in the passenger side window being shattered. Ramon's broken window was not seen as a major issue that would impede the following workday, as he was familiar with the duties of his job, as well as the routes he would take to pick up his workers and their families. Fieldwork, as well as the coordination of it, including the management of several families of workers, was what Jose Ramon dedicated his life to, and he utilized this potential setback as an example to encourage his sons to develop a work ethic like he and the other working families had established.[37] Because of this strong work ethic, elements like a broken window or the coolness of the morning would not and did not impede the workday.

The *Valley Morning Star*'s coverage of the accident. *Courtesy of the City of Alamo Museum.*

The cool morning breeze was persistent, and a trip to Edinburg would be long, so Jose, Raul and Leonel made the decision to cover the fragmented window with a piece of cardboard.[38] Without hesitation, Jose and his two sons boarded the cab of the work truck, with Jose in the driver's seat and his two sons attentively sitting alongside him. Some of the workers would meet at Ramon's property to board the truck, while the others would board as Jose drove through several neighborhoods. The workers had composed themselves early that morning in preparation for the grueling workday ahead. They carried with them jugs of water and sack lunches and wore long-sleeve shirts with heavy, resilient pants and large woven sun hats, which was the usual attire for the workers, as the beating sun and harsh elements would penetrate any fragile clothing.[39]

While Jose and his sons sat in the front of the truck, the back of the truck, covered with a tarpaulin, overflowed with families, conversation and the sound of the howling breeze flowing through and against the open rear. Small children attended the workday with their families as a means of socialization but, most importantly, to keep children cared for when there was nobody else to do so at home. You can only imagine the sound of forty-two people; noise permeated the truck, amplified by the wind and the tarp hitting each other, along with the sounds the truck made as it ventured through various streets, paved or unpaved. Forty-some workers went into the truck, a 1938 Model D-30, six-cylinder, one-and-a-half-ton International Truck, with their supplies and bodies, prepared to work the spring produce fields, but they would never reach the field.

As the Ramons and other working families prepared themselves for the workday, Gulf Coast Lines (now Missouri Pacific) passenger Train No. 113 was traveling westward from Harlingen, Texas, a route described as the "Mission District," which extends from Harlingen to Rio Grande City, a total of 73.3 miles.[40] From a northbound and westbound vehicle view, the intersection of Tower Road and Business 83 was unobstructed.[41]

According to the International Commerce Commission (ICC) report, Ramon's truck possessed "dual rear wheels, a closed cab, and hydraulic brakes. The length of the wheelbase was 155 inches, and the overall length was 244-7/16 inches. The windshield consisted of two sections of glass; each section was 22 inches long and 14 inches high. The windows in each cab door were 15 inches high, 17 inches wide at the top, and 24 inches wide at the bottom. The body of the truck was about 14 feet long and 7 feet wide and 4 feet high and was constructed of wood."[42] Both the train and the work truck were traveling westbound, creating a parallel movement of both engines. Jose Ramon and his workers were using Business 83 or *la calzada grande* to travel from Donna, where most workers had been picked up, with the intention of using Tower Road to travel to the designated field in Edinburg.[43] As Ramon departed Donna, Train No. 113 departed as well, at exactly 8:01 a.m. It had no time to spare, as the arrival times had been backed up, making them one minute late.[44]

That morning, moments before the collision, Train No. 113 was traveling at a speed of forty-five miles per hour on its way from the Donna station to the Alamo station. The track it was on ran parallel to Highway 83, and in the minutes before the crash, it was running parallel to and behind Ramon's truck. As it began to approach the Tower Road crossing, it was, according to some sources, ringing its engine bell and blowing its whistle. It blared its whistle signal for a prolonged period (as was standard operating procedure) as it came closer to the intersection of Tower Road and Business 83. Fireman Garret looked forward along the tracks and saw the truck approaching the intersection. He could see it was slowing down to make a turn right to go north on Tower Road. Garret warned Engineman Wilson of the truck that was going to turn onto the tracks. Wilson shut off the steam and applied the brakes. These actions were fruitless. Because of the train's weight and speed, it was too late to stop, and despite these actions, the train traveled over 1,200 feet west of the crossing, dragging the truck with it.[45]

The impact was directly on the right cab door, hitting and killing Jose Ramon and his sons. Immediately following the impact, the truck itself burst into flames, probably from having a full tank of gas for the journey to the worksite. The train did not catch fire, nor did it have any major damage, and it was able to go on its way after everything was over. However, the heat from the engine and the fire from the truck made the bodies unrecognizable, with parts fusing into the engine of the train. The crash was so powerful that many of those on board were thrown in the air for hundreds of yards on either side of the tracks. Some of the victims also caught fire from the flaming fuel that sprayed on them from the explosion that emanated from the truck.

As the train was attempting to avoid a collision, Mary Ann Wall, secretary of the Alamo Citrus Association, was sitting at her usual workstation, a desk on the east side of the packing plant, which had a perfectly unobstructed view of the Tower Road intersection. Although the Missouri Pacific passenger train traveled this regular route, Wall did not look up to see its passing, as she usually did every time the train made itself known by blaring its horn. When the train crashed into the truck, Wall first noticed the immense cloud of dust that it caused and then a "sheet of flame that burst from the truck." Then she registered that through the sheet of flame, bodies were flying through the dust, flames and rubble, leaving "jumbled heaps along the railroad right-of-way." Wall was at a loss for words; all she could do was open her mouth without letting out a scream. When her boss Albert Jensen, association manager, realized what had happened, he directed her to call "all ambulances in the valley." Because of her witnessing the crash and being the one to call for help, Wall would later be described by Valley newspapers as a "heroine." The Alamo Citrus Association would become a headquarters for newspapermen, ambulances and concerned citizens.[46]

Details from eyewitness reports—such as Wall not looking up to see the passing train as she always did—create a point of contention when trying to determine whether or not the train sounded its horn and the exact actions of Jose Ramon moments before the accident. The one-day investigation that would take place determined that Jose Ramon, the truck driver, was at fault, but these details offer a different perspective: was it a mechanical or human error that resulted in the crash, and if anything, was it not Jose Ramon's fault?

EYEWITNESS STATEMENTS

The events of that tragic day were documented in various newspaper articles and interviews days, years and decades later. Their accounts are stark, honest and graphic; nonetheless, they provide a full account of how horrific the scene was and why it affected all who came upon it for the rest of their lives. Following are the words of these witnesses and survivors.

WITNESS: G.W. Cook, feed and seed store owner who was following Jose Ramon from the nearby city of Donna, Texas. Donna borders Alamo, Texas, on the east. In his testimony at an investigative hearing in Edinburg, the witness described the truck as driving along at a leisurely pace and not attempting to outrun the train. When Ramon made his way to the intersection, he slowed down from forty miles per hour to twenty miles per hour at the intersection, but he did not stop.[47] In fact, in his opinion, the driver of the truck probably did not see the train coming. He goes on to state that the train hit the truck's cab right in the middle of the chassis and that it sounded like an explosion. The impact immediately sent bodies and body parts flying in the air and mixing in with the dust cloud that was sent up with the impact.[48]

WITNESS: Reverend Father P.C. Illigen, pastor of nearby Alamo Catholic Church. Father Illigen made his way to the scene still dressed in his priestly robes and was one of the first persons on the scene. He arrived and began to perform the last rites on the victims, touching his cross to their lips and praying over them. Some of them were his parishioners and so the act was very personal to him. He also attempted to comfort those who were still alive.[49]

WITNESS: McAllen chief of police Noah Cannon. "People stepped on eyeballs and parts of hands and feet as they came in a mad rush to see what happened. Over everywhere there were scattered bits of flesh and body parts."[50]

WITNESS: Espirion Vera, twenty-one years old, farmworker and survivor of the accident.

> We were running along the highway on our way to work in vegetable fields near Edinburg, we turned north on Tower Road on this side of Alamo. I was riding in the rear of the truck. I heard the noise of a train and looked up. The engine bore down upon us, and just before the impact, I jumped. The engine hit the truck broadside with a tremendous impact. Bodies were thrown from the vehicle in every direction. The truck body was reduced to splinters, and the cab was carried down the track.[51]

WITNESS: Guadalupe Hernandez, fourteen years old, farmworker "All I remember is that we were riding to work on the truck. It turned north at the crossing—then there was a loud crash, and I don't remember anything else."[52]

Assistant District Attorney Truman Sanders recounted the words of Engineer Wilson: "Garret [Fireman J.J. Garret] shouted to the engineer that they were going to hit something. Wilson threw on the emergency airbrake and it was set when the engine struck the truck. The impact sounded like we had hit a loaded gasoline drum."[53]

At the time of the accident, witness Rolando Espinoza was helping students cross the street to either Bowie Elementary or St. Joseph's Catholic School on Eighth Street and what is now Business Highway 83. Speaking years later at the age of seventy-three, he stated, "I was standing on the corner crossing with children when I heard a *zumbido* [a loud noise]. It was the first time I saw people in pieces." He and his friend Roberto Trevino immediately knew it was the passenger train because a train would come through on an almost weekly basis bringing what locals referred to as *excursionistas* (people who were brought into the valley to buy land to set up farms). Espinoza said:

These folks came to the valley to buy land and would throw candy out the window to the children. So, my friend and I ran to the train instead of going to school. We ran to see what happened. And the first thing I saw was the truck's front part stuck to the front of the train, all burnt and filled with ashes.

I saw burned body parts stuck to the front of the train and body parts hanging from the side of the train. I immediately thought that the truck belonged to Narciso De Leon, a man from Alamo, but later we found out it wasn't. As I walked, I saw a girl lying on the rails. An older man named Don Julian Macias of Alamo tried sitting her up, but her body went limp like parts of her body were broken. The man told her "Ahorita vienen por ti hijita" [Someone will come for you shortly]. *He tried to console her. Then I found a hand with part of an arm. And it had a golden ring, and the nails had pink nail polish. So, I thought it must have been a girl's.*

He walked down toward the end of the train and saw an African American train employee as well as what he assumed to be the conductor (a white man). As he walked to the end of the six-passenger train, dirt was still in the air from the accident. Walking the length of the train, he was shocked by the scene before him.

I saw all the bodies, like meat you see in Reynosa [a Mexican city just on the other side of the border] *hanging at all the meat markets. I saw a man with his blue overalls lying on his back, hugging a little girl and boy in each arm, dead. I saw a girl who was about ten years old with her little head out on the rail, with her face pushed in as if something had hit her. I saw our German priest Father Illigen talking with a man who was dragging himself with one leg toward his other leg. Father Illigen stopped him and took his confession.*

Espinoza went on to talk about a service given at the Alamo City Park to honor the victims in which the true enormity of all he had witnessed came crashing down on him. He stated, "I can't remember what the priests said at the park, but I could remember I got really nervous and couldn't eat for two weeks."[54]

Brad Smith, a reporter for KRGV radio and the first reporter on the scene, provides one of the most detailed accounts of the immediate aftermath of the accident. Interestingly, this was not the only train accident he was involved in, and years later in 1989, he sat down to tell both of these stories in his personal memoirs. Smith attended Baylor University in Waco, Texas, and really loved athletics, but as he states, he was "too small to play anything but baseball," so he entered the athletic program as an equipment manager, also known as a "water boy." To make some extra money for school, he managed to get a job as a press feeder at the *Baylor University Press* and also earned some paid gigs working for the *Daily Lariat* as a freshman reporter. At the *Daily Lariat*, he met the managing editor, Price Daniels, and struck up a friendship with him that would last the rest of their lives, including working with him on the later-formed Governor's Traffic Safety Committee.

On January 22, 1927, Smith was attending to his work as a press feeder on the day that the Baylor basketball team was to travel to Austin to play against the University of Texas. To be able to attend the game, Brad had made arrangements with driver Joe Potter (who was also a student at Baylor) to drive by the press to pick him up on the team's way out from the university. His plans were shattered momentarily when the foreman, Mr. Hall, walked over to Brad and told him he would need him to work the feeder all day. Smith recalled, "I must have shown major disappointment because he returned a little while later to tell me he would take over my press-feeding job, and he let me off." Smith raced to change his ink-stained shirt and then ran out in hopes to catch the bus, but unfortunately, he saw it pulling away and attempted to chase after it. However, the windows were fogged up and no one could see him chasing after it, so it kept on going down the road. Little did Brad know that missing the bus would save his life.[55]

Aboard the bus were twenty-two young men from the team as well as yell leaders, managers and some fans who were taking the four-hour trip to Austin. The day was rainy, and the driver was traveling through unfamiliar territory when, about three and a half hours into the trip in the town of Round Rock, the bus came across a train crossing. Moving along the tracks was the Sunshine Special, which was racing along because it was behind schedule, reaching speeds of sixty miles per hour, atypical for a train going through a city. The engineer blasted the whistle as he approached the crossing, but no one on board the bus heard the whistle (a commonality in both accidents; could this be a typical refrain after an accident?). Once Potter became aware of the situation, he realized it was too late to apply the brakes, especially on the rain-slicked roads, and decided to attempt to accelerate as fast as he could across the tracks. He also attempted to swerve to the side, and as he did, some students were either thrown or jumped from the bus. The latter half of the bus was still on the tracks when the train collided with it.

Local residents and medical personnel arrived shortly after the accident and rendered what aid they could to the passengers. Nevertheless, ten young men would lose their lives. These young men would forever be remembered as the "Immortal Ten." A fundraising effort of ten years led to them being immortalized in Traditions Square on the Baylor campus in a "ten-by-eight-foot bas-relief panel representing six of the fallen ten athletes. Four free-standing life-sized bronze statues of the remaining athletes complement the panel."[56] It was the worst traffic accident in that decade. Smith and the university community and residents of Waco were in disbelief in the days just after the accident. This memory was carried with Brad Smith when he responded to the call about the accident in Alamo.

What follows are Smith's personal reflections written in 1989 and statements he provided immediately after the accident.

At 8:03 A.M.…I had just stepped from the studios of KRGV Radio at Weslaco, Texas, after finishing my 15-minute morning newscast, when the phone began ringing. I was the News Editor for KRGV, the first full-time radio newsman for any radio station in South Texas south of San Antonio. Grabbing the phone, I heard a frantic man's voice, almost screaming into the phone: "Get down to Alamo quick! There are dead and dying Mexican people all over the place and the engine is on fire!"

Trying to calm the caller down and get a detail or two, I quickly identified the caller was Albert Jensen, manager of the Alamo Fruit Company, a friend long-standing whom I had assisted at the scene of a midnight accident a few weeks earlier. "Albert," I nearly shouted in the excitement of the moment, "you're hollering so loud, I can't understand you! Kinda slow down and tell me where you are and what happened!" Jensen again shouted: "I'm in my office and there's been a terrible wreck right outside my window! If you want a big story, get down here quick! I gotta call doctors and ambulances!" And he slammed the receiver back on the hook as the connection was broken.

I raced out of the station, yelling to the chief engineer, Louis Hartwig, to hurry to the Alamo Fruit Company, eight miles away as fast as possible [with our transcription machine]. I ran to my car and sped to the scene. When I neared Alamo, I saw the regular morning passenger train, stopped at the east side of the town, a small city about halfway between Weslaco, where I worked, and McAllen, where I lived. I drove back and forth between McAllen and Weslaco, sometimes three or four times daily, and had passed Alamo in route to Weslaco for my morning broadcast about an hour and a half earlier, passing several trucks loaded with citrus fruit-

picking crew in route, an every-day occurrence during the citrus harvesting season from October through April, an annual event.[57]

I reached the scene of the collision less than 13 minutes after it had occurred. I ran to the crossing and saw the most horrible sight I have ever witnessed in 13 years of newspaper work in the Valley, except for the 1933 hurricane. Only the hurricane took more lives. I leaped from my car and ran to the crossing. The first sight that met my eyes was a heap of bodies lying on the south side of the railroad track which parallels the highway east and west through the Valley. Horrified, I stopped for a moment to count the bodies. Within a moment or two, I counted 18. Only four of them moved. One man was half lying near the west edge of Tower Road. He was vomiting, and between gasps, he held out his hand piteously for help. I ran to him, and he collapsed. I could do nothing. A few feet away another lay on his face. His clothing was ripped from the back of his body and red welts appeared across his back. He moved a moment or two then laid still.

Running along the railroad right-of-way to the west and almost breathless with horror, I saw arms, legs, and bodies, torn into bits. I saw two arms lying between the rails. The clothing on them was burning. In the midst of the most frightful scene of carnage I have ever seen there was little but stark, horrible death.

I ran westward toward the rear of the train as the first ambulances screamed to a halt. Several hundred feet from the dead and dying, I waved them onto the crossing. I stopped short amazed, as two priests, seemingly appearing from thin air, stepped quietly but swiftly into the scene and began their last administrations.

Most terrifyingly significant throughout those awful first minutes was the fact that so few of the victims—so very few—even so much as moved. It was death on a scale I had never witnessed in this rich peaceful farming country bordering the Rio Grande. The ambulances from a half-a-dozen Valley cities arrived.

I ran up to the front of the train and saw the wreckage of the truck, which the train had carried two blocks from the point of the collision. Two bodies were removed from the pilot of the engine and were so horribly mangled that it was difficult to tell one from the other. The truck had been struck on the right side of the cab, and utterly demolished. It was also badly burned from the fire that followed the collision. One body, caught under the firebox of the engine, was burning fiercely, and the reek of seared flesh nauseated the spectators, who gathered by the thousands.[58]

Within a half-hour of my own arrival, Engineer Hartwig reached the scene with KRGV's portable transcription machine—that was long before the day of cassette recorders or cellular telephones or portable radio broadcasting equipment—set it up and handed me a microphone. I recorded as much information as rapidly as possible on the large discs then in use, and other KRGV employees shuttled them back to Weslaco, where Program Dick Watkins broke into the regular broadcast schedule to broadcast news from Alamo whenever a newly transcribed disc reached the citrus station. The only phone at Alamo Fruit Company's plant office was being used for continuous emergency calls by ambulances, rescue crews, emergency relief personnel, and peace officers. I broadcast in this way throughout the afternoon and into the evening.[59]

Within an hour after the tragedy the Hidalgo County Sheriff's Department, the district attorney's office, and the state highway patrol had investigations underway. Traffic was detoured from the highway during the traffic jam. I believe between four and five thousand people gathered at the scene shortly afterward. Late Thursday, two piles of wreckage—all that was left of the truck—were burned at the scene of the tragedy, twin funeral pyres that marked the worst train-truck collision in Texas history.[60]

These statements provide a detailed testimonial of the events that happened from the impact; however, what happened to cause the accident is still very much open to speculation. Besides his on-the-spot reporting, Brad Smith took several photographs that day, one of which would go on to win a journalism award. The photo was titled "Extreme Unction" and depicts a priest in the middle of all the carnage of the wreck and all the people who had gathered around the scene. The priest is bent over giving comfort to one of the injured on the ground. The photo was entered into the Folmer Craflex Company's golden anniversary contest, and it won first prize out of five thousand entries. It was on display in Rockefeller Center in New York City.[61]

The ICC report presents the following findings:

Engineman Wilson stated that an air-brake test was made at Harlingen and the brakes functioned properly en route. As the train approached Tower Road crossing the engine bell was ringing and he sounded the regulation crossing whistle signal; the last blast was prolonged until the engine reached the crossing. He estimated that the speed was 45 miles per hour and, as he was sounding the last long blast of the whistle, the fireman warned him of a truck approaching the crossing; immediately afterward the collision occurred. He shut off the steam and applied the brakes in an emergency. He said the train stopped about 1,200 feet west of the crossing. The weather was slightly cloudy but visibility was good at the time of the accident, which occurred at 8:06 or 8:07 a.m.

Fireman Garret reiterated Wilson's statements about the brake check and the basic functionality of the brakes and added the following, "When his engine was about 50 or 60 feet from the crossing and while it was moving at a speed of 45 miles per hour, he saw a truck turn from highway U.S. 83 and approach the crossing at a speed of 15 or 20 miles per hour. He immediately warned the engineman, who was still sounding the crossing whistle-signal; the brakes were applied immediately in an emergency and then the accident occurred. He said that the engine struck the truck at the right cab door. He was positive that the window in that door was closed and that the cab was crowded with people. Some sort of covering was over the body of the truck. He said the view of the crossing was unobstructed." Additionally, statements by Roadmaster Stuckey, Agent Reed, and Car Inspector Neely, all asserted that the whistle was sounded, and the brakes were in good condition. Eight nearby residents stated that they heard the whistle.

Mechanical Foreman Schulke stated that after the accident he inspected engine 351 and found the right sill-step of the pilot broken, the left sill-step of the pilot bent, the left injector feed-pipe damaged, and the uncoupling lever on the pilot beam broken. No defect on any car was found and the brakes were in good condition.

George Ingram, Deputy Sheriff, stated that he examined the highway approach to the Alamo crossing and did not observe any skid mark that would indicate the brakes on the truck had been applied. He thought the truck driver had not used the brakes near the crossing involved.

Captain Rose, of the Texas Highway Patrol, stated that he examined the truck after the accident. It was equipped with a rear-view mirror mounted on a 2-foot extension iron to the left of the driver. The window-lift mechanism indicated that both windows were up at the time of the accident. He said that the driver of the truck had a Class P chauffeur's license which indicated that the driver's eyesight had been tested and that he had passed a driving examination in the vehicle which was licensed to drive. He stated that there is no law in the state of Texas requiring a motor vehicle to be stopped before crossing a railroad.

The report provided the following and preceded its conclusion with the following:

There were 41 persons in the truck body. Because of a tarpaulin over the top and the sides of the truck body, these persons could not see in any direction except through the rear end. Three occupants of the body of the truck said they had no warning of the accident. Why the driver failed to observe the approaching train is not known as he was killed in the accident.

The report's conclusion was, "This accident was caused by a motor truck being driven upon a highway grade crossing immediately in front of an approaching train."[62]

When examining any accident, there will always be provable facts and speculation, for there are things that are impossible to know, such as the frame of mind of those involved and even at times those who investigated it. For instance, the statement by Ingram about the fact that there were no skid marks and, therefore, brakes were not applied does not make sense due to the fact that skid marks are only created when brakes are applied quickly and harshly to stop abruptly and not during normal use of brakes. In that light, it seems like an odd statement to make. Perhaps he may have been thinking about if he had seen the train at the last minute and tried to stop, but his statement of "the truck driver had not used the brakes near the crossing" does not seem to support that. Nonetheless, let's explore the truck cab's environment.

Sitting in the front seat of the cab were Jose Ramon and his two sons Leonel and Raul. Where they sat exactly is unknown, but what we can assert is that to the left of Jose Ramon were two people and just past them, the window was covered up by a piece of cardboard due to the attempted break-in. By all reports, it was a cool morning, and covering the window makes sense; they were probably wearing coats. These facts demonstrate that Jose Ramon's view to his right, the direction of the train tracks, was obstructed by both people and cardboard. Also, the noise of the driver, conversations and wind whooshing by (especially since there was no glass but a piece of cardboard sealing the window) would be audible obstructions. In addition, to be able to be hit by the train, he had to have been traveling ahead of the train. These were all factors as to whether he was cognizant of a train on the tracks and how close or far away it was.

We also do not know whether he did know there was a train present and if he was of the mind to attempt to beat it across the tracks. If he was of

Left: Present-day image of the path the train dragged the truck through after the impact. *Courtesy of Juan Carmona.*

Below: Present-day image of the intersection where the crash occurred. *Courtesy of Juan Carmona.*

that mind, that idea may have occurred perhaps in a regular car, but he was driving a large truck, the back of which had a bed that contained the weight of over forty people, not to mention that he had two of his sons right next to him in the cab. That makes the idea of him attempting to beat the train a little less likely, but once again, we will never know. In the end, what he saw or did not see as he approached the intersection and made his fateful turn died with him.

Those Whose Lives Were Lost Due to the Accident
Adelfina Alaniz, thirteen
Amador Garza, twenty-one
Manuel Gonzales, fourteen
Matias Gonzales, fourteen
Pedro Grimaldo, thirty-three
Adalberto Munoz, fourteen
Anival Munoz, ten
Carmen Perez, twelve
Estevan Perez, twenty-nine
Juan Perez, thirty
Otila Perez, twenty-five
Victoria Perez, twelve
Jose Ramon, forty-two
Leonel Ramon, eighteen
Nuverto Ramon, twenty-seven
Raul Ramon, sixteen
Anastacia Rosa, eighteen
Benita Alvarado Rosa, fifty
Claudia Rosa, eleven
Emerencia Rosa, forty
Juan Rosa, thirty-eight
Leonora (Leonor) Rosa, thirty-eight
Maria Rosa, thirteen
Oralia Rosa, seventeen
Ruben (Rodriguez) Rosa, twenty-four
Salvador Vera, twenty-one
Fidel Villareal, eight
Josefa Villareal, thirteen
Manuel Villareal, eighteen

PART III

AFTERMATH

DIRECT IMPACTS AND RESPONSE

A few blocks north of the Business 83 and Tower Road intersection was the Mexican neighborhood of Acacia Street. When the Missouri Pacific train struck Jose Ramon's truck of workers, the community that worked and lived near Acacia Street was the first to hear the impact of the crash. Living within a few blocks of the intersection was twelve-year-old Donaciano Garza, the son of a butcher and usual helper in his father's business. At the time of the accident, at approximately 8:06 a.m. on March 14, 1940, Donaciano was attending to his father's work tasks, butchering goats and other animals. Their morning work was interrupted by the loud sound of a steel train colliding with the truck. The sound was so loud that Donaciano's father knew something terrible had occurred and ordered his son not to go and see what had resulted from the crash.

As a curious and rebellious young child, Donaciano ignored his father and took off from his shop, running all the way to the crash site. Upon arrival at the crash site, Donaciano was stopped, as others were, by the adults who had arrived first to render aid and collect the debris and bodies that scattered the railroad. Two blocks of bodies and debris are what Donaciano, now in his nineties, distinctly remembers. Days and weeks following the accident were occupied by the collective action of the community in cleaning the railroad area, as well as gathering any remaining body pieces. According to Donaciano, weeks after the accident, body parts were still being found. Following the accident, the community members also added their opinions about what had happened; what Donaciano heard from the adults is that the

The aftermath of the train accident. *Courtesy of Laura Elizalde.*

driver, Jose Ramon, attempted to speed up to cross the tracks but was instead met by the Missouri Pacific.[63]

Mr. Hinojosa, a relative of the Perez family victims and survivors, still has trouble retelling the stories passed down from grandfather to father and to him, illustrating the impact the story still has on him. Hinojosa notes that it was hard for any stories to be passed down until he himself retired at sixty-two years old and his father began to open up to him. The story begins as Hinojosa's father was attempting to identify the remains of relatives of theirs, which were then put into caskets and prepared to be taken to the receiving families. In El Sauz, Texas, a town not too far from Rio Grande City, Hinojosa's grandfather owned land that contained fields on which his grandfather was working when trucks of caskets (he did not initially see the caskets) approached him with various individuals asking where he wanted *los muchachos* (the children), his siblings. Hinojosa's grandfather was not aware of what had happened the day earlier, on March 14, and thought that these individuals meant where did he want his siblings to go, as he was working on his land. In response, Hinojosa's grandfather responded, "Dile a Nacha que les halgo de comer," meaning to tell his wife to prepare something for them to eat. Hinojosa's grandfather was not expecting to be met with the bodies of his loved ones and instead thought they had come home unexpectedly, prompting his wife, Nacha, to make some food.[64]

Many of the surviving children of the families affected by the crash were met not only with the immense loss of their relatives but were also faced with forced relocation, as many of their older siblings and adults had perished in the crash. The older siblings who did survive or were not involved in the actual crash had to become surrogate parents, merging their newfound parenthood and personal lives into makeshift families. The Ramon family faced many obstacles after the death of the truck driver and patriarch, Jose Ramon. One story is told by Israel Ramon Jr., whose father was one of the oldest sons of Jose Ramon and was supposed to be in the truck that day but due to his not having had a haircut was left behind. Israel Jr. describes that his father began to consider his brothers and sisters as his own children upon moving into the same house as one of the older surviving daughters, as all the younger siblings became their responsibility, in addition to the growth of their own families. This tightknit family grew in one small house on South Missouri Street in Weslaco, also referred to as "South Mo." Because of this, Israel Jr. grew up directly with his cousins, whom he considered his own siblings. His cousin Richard Cortez was the son of one of the eldest daughters, who acted as the surrogate mother for the Ramon family, as her brother Israel Sr. acted as the surrogate father.[65]

Jose Ramon Jr. was one of the children who had to be taken in by his older brother and his older sister along with her husband. At the time of the accident, he was only five years old. In his personal recount of the day, his family experienced the worst loss imaginable. He remembers his mother sobbing, as she had just lost her husband and two sons and unfortunately would later pass herself. One of the most significant memories that Jose Ramon Jr. has even now is that whenever his father, the driver of the truck, would work around the Valley, and even in fields outside the Valley, he would always bring little toys and keepsakes for young Jose Jr., as he was one of the youngest children. Work as a mayordormo often meant leaving for long periods of time, which made these toys and gifts even more special, as it marked the return of a loved one after a long time apart. This memory offers insight into viewing those who bring food to our tables as more than just laborers, but humans, with families and priorities that often go unnoticed because of the demand of the profession.[66]

Hidalgo County judge Richard Cortez, grandson of truck driver Jose Ramon. *Courtesy of Juan Carmona.*

Ricardo Felipe Cortez is a very recognizable name in Hidalgo County, which is the county in which Alamo is located. He led the county through the national crisis that was COVID-19. It was his name on the proclamations that laid out county curfews, lockdown orders, mask mandates and the final lifting of them. Judge Cortez was at the forefront of efforts to combat the spread of the virus as well as dealing with the consequences of such large numbers of loss of life, ending in the ordering of refrigerated trucks to handle the overflow of bodies that the local morgues and mortuaries could not handle. He had to deal with people who did not believe the virus was real, but he persevered, serving his community to the best of his ability. Undoubtedly, the residents of Hidalgo County know Judge Cortez, but most do not know his connection to the Alamo train accident.

When the authors first reached out to Judge Cortez's office to request an interview and state the purpose of the said interview, we received a response from his assistant stating that we had just educated them about their boss. This will probably be the same reaction from his constituents when this book comes out, but he is very open about his family's connection and shared openly at the most recent commemoration ceremony and with the authors of this book. Richard Cortez is the grandson of Jose Ramon, the driver of the truck involved in the accident, and he and his family grew up in the aftermath of the accident.

Cortez was not born until 1943, but he would hear about the accident through his mother, who was the oldest of the remaining nine siblings of the Ramon family. Her name was Natalia Ramon Cortez. Upon her marriage to Cortez's father, the two became the surrogate parents of the rest of the siblings. They all lived in a house in Weslaco. They had moved to Weslaco from their home in East Donna when his mother got married. The house was very crowded. As you would walk in through the front door, there was a bedroom that housed Cortez's three single aunts. The next room contained a bedroom where his three single uncles lived, and the next one was the one bathroom that the whole family had to share. In the next bedroom was his one married uncle, the father of Israel Ramon. In the back of that house was a small two-story annex to the home, in which on the first floor lived Richard Cortez and his mother and father and on the top floor lived another married uncle. Although the whole family lived in what could be considered cramped conditions, Cortez points out that they had a happy life. He never felt poor or deprived of any wants or needs; to them, that was their life, and they were happy. Like most Mexican families, the family was the center of their lives, and it was how they held each other up and made it through the worst of times.

Judge Cortez credits his family's survival and the later success of his family to his mother, whom he describes as strong-willed. His mother and father were always working along with his older uncles Israel and Modesto, who worked hard so that the younger siblings could go to school. His uncle Israel worked as a truck driver, transporting farmworkers as his father did. Agriculture and cotton were the main industries in the Rio Grande Valley at that time. His father would go on to own a Texaco service station. They would also go on to own and operate a small grocery store. One of his other uncles found work as a customs officer.

His mother was also very involved with the local Catholic church and became friends with one of the priests of the church, Father Frank Kilday. Father Kilday's brother was the sheriff of Bexar County (an area that encompasses the San Antonio area) and was friends with Joe Kilgore, a congressman in Washington, D.C. These connections his mother had through the church allowed her to ask Father Kilday's assistance in getting a good education for her younger siblings. He, in turn, had his brother request assistance from Kilgore, and as a result, Cortez's uncle Joe Jr. (son of Jose Ramon) was admitted into St. Mary's University in San Antonio. She was also able to facilitate her other sibling Romeo (Rey) Cortez being admitted to Georgetown University in Washington, D.C., and he went on to work for Kilgore in Capitol Hill. They were the first ones in the family to graduate from college. Jose, Romeo and the rest of the siblings went on to start new and successful lives, all as a direct result of the actions of his mother, Natalia.

Judge Cortez was a graduate of Weslaco High School and attended Pan American College in Edinburg, Texas (today University of Texas Rio Grande Valley). He majored in accounting at the college, but during his time in school, he had already begun to work for an accounting firm in Weslaco, earning him real-world experience in his chosen field. As a result, the minute he graduated and passed his Certified Public Accountant (CPA) exam, he was hired as a CPA. He began by doing tax returns for small to midsize businesses in the Valley. He also worked as an auditor for different municipalities. As he moved forward in his career, he became an expert in economic damages, meaning he would be the one to calculate damages for lawsuits or defend the calculations of others in lawsuits.

He did that for about forty years of his life, and at age sixty-one, when all his kids were grown, it was time to devote himself to the community. He ran for mayor in the city of McAllen and won the election, serving as mayor for eight years, after which his wife asked him to step down and not run again so they could spend time together. Unfortunately, a year and a half later, she passed away, leaving him a widower with a lot of time on his hands. So, he decided to return to public service, and he ran for and was elected city commissioner. He then went on to be elected Hidalgo County judge, in which capacity he still serves to this day.

Serving as county judge, Cortez was able to fully appreciate the issues Hidalgo County was facing. One that really stood out to him was the fact that so many families were living in poverty. In a meeting with Workforce Solutions, he was presented with the fact that 27 percent of children in the county were living with food insecurity. This issue was only exacerbated by the COVID-19 epidemic; that number jumped from 27 percent in 2018 to 37 percent in 2020. He was startled by these numbers, and those numbers became real when he opened a Boys and Girls Club in Pharr, Texas, and there he observed a young girl with a plate of food who ate only one section of the plate and asked if she could take the rest home so that her brothers and sisters could have something to eat. Cortez has gone on to create a task force, the Prosperity Task Force of Hidalgo County, to study the underlying issues, such as lack of education and job training, and looks to find a solution.

Members of the Ramon family like Judge Cortez and Israel Ramon found success after the tragedy in Alamo; this demonstrates the resiliency of their family and the larger South Texas community.[67]

THE ROSAS

The Rosa family experienced the largest loss of family members, losing nine members in total. Isabel Rosa Pena, daughter of Emerencio Rosa and Benita Alvarado, became an orphan at the age of seven due to the Alamo train-truck crash. Isabel recounts the day as a "muggy" Thursday morning on which Jose Ramon "made the error of his life." Isabel was the youngest of a large family of eight children, plus her two parents, so when the opportunity to work in the field was offered, it was considered a "deal of a lifetime"; money was much needed, and the older siblings could contribute to the family through their labor in the fields. The youngest children were left at home, so Modesta, the eldest, was the one to take care of them and the house as the parents and other children would go work. During that early Thursday morning of March 14, Modesta was at home doing the family's laundry and taking care of the youngest children. The radio station began broadcasting breaking news on a major accident that had occurred at a railroad crossing in Alamo. Isabel remembers hearing people crying and discussing the scene of the crash; body parts were scattered everywhere, "pieces of organs and skin smothered" on the train and the redness of the road due to large amounts of blood. It was so horrifying that a priest called to give the victims their last rites suffered a heart attack.

When the bodies of Isabel's loved ones—her parents, siblings, uncle, aunt and cousin—were finally brought home, the cost and difficulty of burying them was not the only challenge, as "some adult" decided that all the younger siblings had to go to an orphanage. The mourning process was met with the

Members of the Rosa family, *left to right*: Emerencio Rosa, Simona Rosa and Juan Rosa. *Courtesy of Patricia Rosa.*

confusion and fear of becoming an orphan and the risk of being separated from the only family they had left. To avoid the harsh and quick separation of the children, Modesta had to absorb the family as the sole provider. She earned money by cleaning houses, washing clothes and ironing for several rich families. Isabel remembers everything being so expensive that to have clothes for school, Modesta would use flour sacks. Isabel, as an older woman, gives credit to her older sister Modesta for setting an example of loyalty and responsibility to her family. She, along with her sister Paula Rosa Alaniz, also remembers the instability that ensued after the crash—moving from house to house, in which some foster homes would require them to work in order to eat. The Rosa family was so affected that many members of the family began to tattoo their names onto their arms to be identified if an accident with the same destruction were to happen again. Isabel became a strong woman because of the loss of half her family, as well as her relatives, and emphasized that learning and keeping the stories of our ancestors are of the utmost importance.[68]

The following information was put together via interviews with different descendants of the Rosa family. Those interviewed were Dagoberto Rosa Salinas, son of Catarina Rosa; Joel Rosa, son of Santos Rosa; and Patricia Rosa, daughter of Anecleto Rosa.

Catarina, Santos and Anecleto Rosa lost both their parents—their father, Juan Rosa, and mother, Leonor Rosa—and their two older sisters, Oralia and Claudia Rosa. At the time of the train crash, Catarina was six years old, Santos (who was in the accident) was eight and Anecleto, the youngest, was eighteen months old. Catarina and Anecleto were back home in Garceño (in Starr County) with their grandmother, as they were too young to work and stayed behind with her. The grandmother Braulia Rosa worked at the time as a *partera* (midwife) for women in the community.

The orphans went through real financial hardship as they grew up, as well as a harsh and sometimes physically abusive environment at home. At

Caskets of train wreck victims being taken into Lutheran Church at Escobares for funeral

Caskets being taken into Escobares Cemetary for fena burial

The arrival of the caskets bearing the bodies of some of the victims of the crash being taken to their funeral in Escobares, Texas. *Courtesy of the City of Alamo Museum.*

the time of the accident, their father had large tracts of land and cattle in his name. Their uncles and grandmother saw the young orphans as "commodities" due to their father's lands and the money that was set aside for them by the train company. In time, they exploited their inheritance, taking the lands and money for themselves. When the oldest orphaned daughter, Juanita Rosa, celebrated her fifteenth birthday, a time when most young girls would celebrate with a *quinceañera* (a large coming-of-age celebration), she was instead taken to the bank to sign over her money to her uncles at the behest of Braulia Rosa. In time, they would also obtain ownership of their father's lands, leaving the orphaned siblings with nothing. Also, the uncles would make the surviving boys work all day in the fields from sunup to sundown with no pay whatsoever.

Later, when Anecleto was an adult and was married, he began to fight his uncles to get some of the land back. It was a difficult fight due to the nature of landownership at the time; he did not have deeds to fall back on due to everything being mostly done via word of mouth. Additionally, he did not have very much support within the family, so it was an arduous journey. The fight would last sixteen years, and in the end, he was finally awarded only six acres back. He would go on to divide it into portions for his siblings (three girls and three boys who were left behind) to have some property for themselves.

The graves of some members of the Rosa family located in Escobares. *From left to right*: Ruben Rodriguez, Claudia Rosa, Leonor Rosales and Juan Rosa. *Courtesy of Taylor Seaver*.

Rosa family gravestones in Escobares. *From left to right*: Anastacia Rosa, Oralia Rosa, Emerencia Rosa, Benita Alvarado, Paula Rosa and Maria Rosa. *Courtesy of Taylor Seaver*.

The fight for the land, his maltreatment as a child and the raw emotions attached to all of it left a huge emotional scar on Anecleto. He would rarely speak about it, and with time, he medicated himself with alcohol. Even to this day, he refuses to talk about the accident and what followed. On the day of this interview, Patricia Rosa had a hard time trying to get more information out of him. He became upset and would not speak more on the subject. The family has been trying to get him to see the historical marker of the crash (he currently resides north of the Rio Grande Valley, in Corpus Christi, Texas), but he refuses to go.

Eventually, Catarina would get married and have children, but her husband ended up leaving the family when Dagoberto was only two years old. Once again, she found herself alone and struggling. In the early 1960s, there was no financial assistance for families or food stamps, so the family relied on their local food pantry to help put food on the table. Nevertheless, she persevered, and her strength got their family through the hard times.

Joel Rosa's father, Santos Rosa, survived the accident. He was seated toward the open back of the truck. When the initial impact of the train occurred, his father, Juan Rosa, was seated next to him and pushed him out

Members of the Rosa family, *from left to right*: Joel Rosa, Dagoberto Rosa Salinas and Irma Rosa Perez. *Courtesy of Juan Carmona.*

of the truck, and he fell on his back. His back landed on another set of tracks running parallel to the set that the train was on. The impact left him with a large scar across his back, which he would show to his son and his cousin. Due to the accident, he was in the hospital for a year, and no one from the family knew he was still alive.

Santos was initially told by people at the hospital that he was probably never going to be able to walk again, but he fought hard and pushed himself to be able to walk. Santos's time in the hospital was made a little less isolating through his connection with a kind nurse with whom he formed an almost mother-son relationship. Due to his young age, he sought a mother figure to help him make it through the tragedy and his physical suffering. It was this woman who truly exemplified the role of a nurse, serving both this boy's physical and emotional needs. Although the family does not recall her name, they are indebted to this compassionate woman. Santos never really talked much about the accident and the aftermath; it was too painful a subject for him to dwell on. They did hear him talk about it a little bit when someone approached him to let him know that they were placing a monument at the crash site. Joel learned more from his uncles who would talk about what happened.

AFTERMATH

Ambulances from Edinburg, McAllen and Mercedes were en route after the crash occurred. As the remains were collected, there were also some immediate survivors who were transported to several hospitals around the Valley. City Hospital in McAllen, Texas, was the site to which many of the injured victims were taken.[69]

According to the *Delphos Daily Herald*, many of the injured and initial survivors of the accident were taken to the hospital, but "physicians were handicapped by lack of space," and according to Charles King, an ambulance driver, within an hour six bodies were at McAllen Funeral Home, eight bodies in Weslaco and some in Edinburg. Further newspaper reports describe similar circumstances.[70] According to the *McAllen Daily Press*, thirteen "complete" bodies were taken to Kriedler mortuary in McAllen, and other complete bodies were taken to Martin-Wilson in Weslaco. The *McAllen Daily Press* also noted that about sixteen individuals were taken to McAllen Municipal Hospital and were "undergoing treatment":

> Adelfina Alaniz
> Jesus Alaniz, nine
> Pedro Alaniz, thirteen
> A. Gomez, sixteen
> Juana Gonzalez, seventeen
> Guadalupe Hernandez, fourteen
> Faustino Perez, nine

Jose Perez, forty-three
Anastacia Rosa
Juan Rosa, thirty-two
Santos Rosa, eight
Espiridion Vera, twenty-one
Josefa Villarreal, thirteen
Jose Villarreal, eighteen
Leonel Villarreal, fifteen
One unidentified individual[71]

McAllen's hospital building was first built in 1920; it was a two-story structure, combined with a home and office, owned by Dr. J.M. Doss. In 1925, just fifteen years prior to the crash, the first municipal hospital was built on South Broadway, with beds for twenty-five patients. It would soon become overwhelmed with demand for more space. In 1928, to meet population growth and medical demands, a new hospital was built on Main Street, connecting to the older structure with a covered passageway; additions were later added in 1954, 1960, 1967 and 1973.[72]

About a week after the crash, eight victims were still in the hospital, though the hospital released that during this time, victims were in "satisfactory conditions"; Espiridion Vera, Pedro Alaniz, A. Gamez and Lionel Villarreal were released that Thursday.[73] Two weeks following the crash, victims Faustina Perez and Santos Alanis were dismissed, while four others were still hospitalized for injuries sustained in the crash and Santos Rosa was in critical condition.[74] Leonora Rosa and her daughter Claudia were not immediately laid to rest together, as there was a delay in the identification of the bodies by family members.[75] This gives some sense of the amount of body identification done by the Rosa family and the intensity of the bodily injuries sustained by the victims.

As mentioned previously in the testimony of Donaciano Garza, the collection of the victims' body parts was a task that was not completed within the first days following the crash or even weeks after, but instead was an ongoing process as parts were continually being found. Costales, or sacks, used to collect the picked produce by fieldworkers was what Imelda notes in her testimony as what her father and grandfather used to collect the human remains. This demonstrates the extreme physics involved in the accident and the difficulty for the families knowing that many of their relatives' body parts were not recovered easily or could not be recovered at all. At the time of the crash, Francisco Gomez and his son Victoriano were part of the recovery effort. Imelda, the daughter of Victoriano Gomez, recalls that since there were so many human remains scattered along the railroad, anyone who could help was called. Imelda's grandfather at the time worked for the City of Alamo, so he and other city workers were asked to collect the remains immediately after the crash had occurred. Imelda notes that this task left a significant mark in her grandfather's and father's memories, as it was a heartbreaking moment in their lives and careers.[76]

In the days following the train-truck crash, the community united to pay their respects to the lives lost. Florence Scott, county school superintendent, ordered all schools closed on Friday so that teachers could assist the orphans and families of the victims. Some teachers ended up taking in some students temporarily so that they could provide food and shelter. Others purchased and/or donated items of food and clothing to the victims and their families. According to the *Brownsville Herald*, the days following the accident were dedicated to a memorial service and mass for the victims and survivors. It was noted that "more than 3,000 persons" attended the memorial service hosted at Alamo City Park. The mass was given on Monday morning by Reverend Peter C. Illigen, pastor of St. Joseph's, who was one of the first persons to reach the scene of the accident, administering extreme unction or anointing of the sick to the dying victims. In an article honoring the remembrance of the crash, KVEO-TV includes that eighty-one-year-old Sixto Villarreal remembered the accident as something that took four of his father's cousins, stating that "there was a rosary and mass every Saturday."

THE LEGAL SYSTEM

That fateful morning of March 14 would leave many families with huge holes where their loved ones once had been. Sadly, those who remained behind were hit with some significant practicalities to the loss because many had lost their breadwinners, parents, brothers and sisters. In farm-working families, the more family members who could assist in fruit picking or other types of work meant more money for the household, and now many were missing and the struggles were exacerbated. There were many who would be approached by lawyers who would attempt to get some sort of settlement from the railroad company. However, the major obstacle that they would be faced with is the fact that the one-day investigation by Judge Slaughter, the Interstate Commerce Commission and the State Railroad Commission ended with the same conclusion, stated here by C.F. Boulton:

> The accident was caused by the truck being driven upon the railroad crossing immediately in front of the incoming passenger train. The crossing was found to be in good condition, the train brakes working, and the train operating within the permitted speed of 45 miles per hour. A standard warning sign was recorded at the crossing. There was also a finding that the train engineer blew the proper whistle signals at the crossing. It is obvious the driver of the truck did not see the train in time to avoid the accident.[77]

Placing the blame on Jose Ramon's inattention made it difficult to place any responsibility on the railroad company or the state. These conclusions were drawn within a day or two of the accident, which leads one to question their accuracy or thoroughness; nevertheless, this is what any lawyer and their claimant would have to face when they entered the courtroom.

Not all lawyers who sought out families who had someone who perished in the accident or those who were injured had altruistic motives. There was some concern about some of these families being taken advantage of by unscrupulous attorneys. The Mexican Consulate appointed attorney Ramon Longoria to "investigate all the legal phases" of the accident and its impact on the families. With utmost concern for the families, the consulate issued a statement that all those involved in the accident, families of the victims and those injured should "not sign any papers or make any settlements without consulting consular officials." It was crucial to have a lawyer review their contracts so that proper fees and percentages were being charged before anything was signed and they became attached to an attorney.[78]

It is important to note that in 1940, the United States was adhering to its Good Neighbor Policy, which was laid forth in a 1938 speech by then-president Franklin D. Roosevelt:

> *In the field of world policy, I would dedicate this Nation to the policy of the good neighbor—the neighbor who resolutely respects himself and, because he does so, respects the rights of others—the neighbor who respects his obligations and respects the sanctity of agreements in and with a world of neighbors. We now realize as we have never realized before our interdependence on each other; that we cannot merely take but must give as well.[79]*

This policy was reflective of the fact that the United States was attempting to foment good relations between the nations of the Americas in which all interactions between nations would be mutually beneficial. Additionally, the year of the accident being 1940 means that World War II was raging in Europe, and Roosevelt knew that the United States would eventually be dragged into the conflict. He was especially cognizant that the Good Neighbor Policy would also help to prevent any kind of German intrigue along the border. So, Mexico did have a strong standing in its advocating for the fair treatment of Mexicans and Mexican Americans.

Nonetheless, the Mexican Consulate was not the only entity concerned with irregularities or people being taken advantage of; there was also the Mexican American civil rights organization El Congreso de Pueblos de Habla Española (the Spanish Speaking People's Congress), referred to by most as simply El Congreso. This organization was first created in response to combat issues faced by the Mexican American community, the biggest being violence by the Ku Klux Klan as well as by state actors. Formed in California in 1935, it would remain active until the 1950s and would spread across the Southwest from California to Texas. It would grow to 120 chapters with approximately 1,500 members. Despite how prolific it became, it was eventually dissolved in 1950 during the Red Scare, when most organizations like this were accused of being communists.[80]

However, in 1940, El Congreso was still going strong, and on March 16, 1940, then-president Manuel Trevino and vice president Pedro B. Hernandez organized a meeting at Union Hall in San Antonio. The meeting was attended by over one thousand people, a demonstration of the larger impact of the story and the concern of the Mexican American community. During the meeting, the group questioned the length of the investigation, calling it "not sufficient to bring out the details of the tragedy," and stated that "the very nature of this accident reveals the unsafe conditions in which workers are transported to the fields with men, women, and children into trucks." As a result, the organization called for then–Texas governor W. Lee O'Daniel to conduct a "detailed and thorough investigation" to root out all the factors that led to this tragic incident.[81] To the group and others, the driver simply not paying attention was not a sufficient answer to what exactly happened that horrible morning.

On the morning of March 31, the first lawsuits were filed at the Hidalgo County Courthouse. The first claimants were Eva Resendez De Perez, Trinidad Perez and Canuto Perez. Eva Perez was there as the representative party for her husband, Esteban Perez, who was killed in the accident. She was also acting on behalf of her three children, three-year-old Benita, two-year-old Ubaldo and two-month-old Guillermo. Additionally, she was suing for herself directly. The suit sought $30,000 for the wife and children and another $10,000 for the parents of Esteban. Through their attorneys, they alleged ten acts of negligence on behalf of the railway company. The attorneys, all from San Antonio, were from the firm of Shlesinger, Shlesinger, and Goodstein, and from outside the firm, there was J.D. McGuire and the additional firm of Hill and Oliver.[82]

Some of their claims of negligence were the following: One, that the train was not "maintained under proper control." Second, "failure to keep a proper lookout stationed at the point of the crash." Next, "failure to ring the locomotive bell." Also, "failure to blow the whistle as required by law" (a point of continuous contestation due to conflicting reports on this issue).

Finally, it charged "operation of the train at an excessive rate of speed."[83] This last charge probably comes from the fact that an examination of the rail schedule revealed that it was running behind schedule and therefore may have been traveling at a higher speed than usual as it approached the city of Alamo, despite the fact that trains are supposed to slow down as they enter populated areas. Trinidad Perez, age seventeen, filed his own suit, asking $20,000 and claiming similar incidents of negligence as the previous suit, as well as claims of injury to his back, head, spine, feet and hips that were going to leave the young man permanently disabled and thus unable to work. Shortly after these filings, it was announced by local Donna law firm Walter G. Weaver and Son that it had also obtained two clients in connection to the accident.[84]

The Weavers would go on to contract with eleven different plaintiffs regarding the accident. One of the families who contracted with him was the Ramon family, suing on behalf of the family for Jose Ramon and his two sons Raul and Leonel, all three of whom perished in the accident. Another client they picked up in association with the accident was Julio Garcia, also of Donna, who had suffered a broken arm because after he was thrown from the vehicle he was struck by the torso of another victim, a testament to the violent forces within the accident.[85] Ramon's widow, Natividad F. Ramon, was seeking via her lawyers a total of $50,500. This total came from her suit for the life of her husband, in which she asked for $10,000; $500 for the loss of the truck; and $40,000 for the children's loss of their father.[86]

In April of the same year, two more suits were filed by attorneys representing Braulia Rosa, who was asking for a total of $50,000 for the loss of her son Juan Rosa. Another suit was filed by Modesta Cortez, who was also seeking $50,000 on behalf of the six children of Emerencia Rosa.[87] Later that same month, twelve more suits were filed at the Ninety-Second District Court. The suits came from the following families: Prospero Vera for the death of his son Salvador Vera. Esperion Vera claimed $10,000 for injuries he suffered in the accident. Enrique and Romula Munoz were seeking $20,000 for the death of their two sons Anival and Alberto. Daniel Villarreal filed as "the next best friend" (a legal term used for someone who represents the interest of another who is either incapacitated, incompetent or a minor) of his son Leonel Villarreal for the death of Leonel's son Daniel. Eusebia Villarreal asked for $10,000 for the deaths of her two sons Manuel and Fidel, as well as the death of her daughter Josefa. Eusebio G. Villarreal filed a claim on behalf of his daughter Guadalupe for injuries sustained in the accident. Jorge Perez filed for $32,000 in the death of his daughter

Carmen; $10,000 for his daughter Faustina, who sustained injuries in the accident; and his son Pedro and himself, who were injured in the accident.[88]

Later in December, three suits were filed: one by Atadio Gamez asking for $10,000 for his injuries and an additional $250 for medical bills and to pay for his medications; another by Santos Rosa, who was nine at the time and had a representative file on his behalf for the sum of $10,000 for injuries and $200 in medical bills; and finally, Gregorio Alanis for himself and his two children for $45,000—$10,000 for the death of his daughter Delfina, $5,000 for injuries sustained by his son Pedro and another $15,000 for injuries received by his son Jesus. All of these were filed against Guy A. Thompson as trustee for the railroad company.[89]

The first suit made its way to the empaneling of a grand jury involving Eva Resendez, who filed for herself and her three children Benito, Ubaldo and Guillermo, who were suing for $40,000 in the death of her husband, Esteban Perez. Judge Bryce Ferguson organized the grand jury for the month of September. The priority for the grand jury was criminal offenses. District attorney Tom L. Hartley had more than twenty cases to put before the jury, including cases on drug possession, murder, forgery and driving while intoxicated. Those cases would be presented before the jury on the first Monday and Tuesday of the month, followed by civil cases, which would be those related to the train-truck accident.[90] Once the grand jury received the testimony, then they would forward the cases toward a court date.

In the end, for all the claimants involved, it would be months from the initial date of the first suits until the day a settlement was made. The grand total sum of all the lawsuits was $679,525 against the railroad representative Thompson.[91] Unfortunately for the families, on December 2, 1940, a settlement was reached between all the lawyers involved in forty-two cases. In the end, the railroad and the lawyers settled on a grand total of $28,000 for everyone. If split evenly, that would be approximately $666.70 per plaintiff. This award was to be used by the families to pay for burial and medical expenses, which Thompson did not cover. Upon reaching the settlement, Thompson issued a statement on behalf of the railroad company stating that "in paying the agreed judgments, [the railroad] assumed no liability."[92] It is no doubt that all the investigations faulting the driver, Jose Ramon, as the responsible party in the accident played a key role in such a small judgment being received by the claimants. The authors were not able to find any reference to additional investigations as called for by El Congreso, so there was not much for the families' lawyers to work with to exact a higher cost.

Whatever hopes and dreams the parties involved were looking forward to were crushed. They were once again left with the emptiness and fears of what to do now. They were still missing their breadwinners; others were too injured to work, and many would carry psychological scars from the incident. For them, there would be no solace, just a simple retreat within themselves to find a way to survive.

FUNDRAISING EFFORTS

As is usually the story of disasters or major accidents like the subject of this book, people band together to support their community. A group of Valley-area Mexican priests created a fund to help the victims, known as the Alamo Memorial Fund. The fund began with some initial donations that added up to $300. One of the first major fundraisers was the sale of 960 pounds of Grand Champion Beef from the Houston Stock Show. It was purchased by the manager of the Grand Prize Brewing Company and auctioned off, netting $1,000 for the memorial fund.[93] There was also a host of different charity shows to benefit the victims, including one hosted by the Mexican Consulate that raised $124.[94]

In Brownsville, Texas, there was a large variety show held at El Tiro theater that consisted of a one-act play and a series of films, including the film *Bajo el Cielo de México*, a feature film depicting life in Mexico and the headliner of the night. The event was organized by Mexican consul Carlos A. Calderon and some of Brownsville's most prominent families, who arranged for all the services provided to be donated for use at the event. It was a late-night program, beginning at 11:00 p.m. Besides the play and films, there was musical entertainment and a brief talk by Calderon highlighting the purpose of the night, to support the victims of the Alamo accident.[95] In the end, the show would go on to net $320.50 for the victims and their families.[96]

The American Red Cross spent two weeks assessing the needs of the victims and their families. The investigation was led by Edith Hennesey of the St. Louis branch of the organization. At the end of the two weeks,

Hennesey held a meeting at the McAllen Chamber of Commerce office and presented their recommendation for a maintenance fund for the families. The disbursement of funds would be led by the two local chapters of the Red Cross, which would distribute payments to the families from a $2,000 fund. This support would last up to one year.[97] These funds would be targeted at those families who had lost their main breadwinners and had no real means of supporting themselves.

The sum of all these efforts and the lawsuit money helped some of the families through the lean times that occurred directly after the accident as they were dealing with funeral costs, medical bills and a severe loss of income. Many were left scrambling to find places to live and how to put food on the table. It was a real struggle for families who were already struggling to survive day to day; now they were dealt yet another hurdle in life, so any help was needed and appreciated.

TRAFFIC SAFETY PROGRAM

An indirect result of the crash was something that came about years later, on January 15, 1957, when Texas Governor Price Daniel decided to create the Governor's Traffic Safety Commission. Governor Daniel's interest in traffic safety arose from the death of his aunt, who was killed in a car accident as she was on her way home from the governor's inauguration. This pet project of the governor would be run out of his office, and he would enlist newsman Brad Smith to help with this endeavor. The governor reached out to Smith because he was a friend of Daniel's and he believed his experience in newsprint, radio and now television would make for a perfect spokesperson who knew how to engage with the public. Plus, due to his connection with previous accidents like the Alamo crash, he already had experience advocating for traffic safety. Smith was excited to be offered the position; however, it would mean his quitting KRGV and moving from the Valley to Austin.

As part of this initiative, the Texas Department of Public Safety (DPS) provided the governor with a report with information about traffic accidents within the past five years. For those previous five years, the state averaged approximately 2,500 traffic deaths per year. The study went on to point out that the major causes of death were drinking and driving as well as road conditions. Both accounted for about 80 percent of all fatalities in Texas.

This DPS report gave the governor the information he would need to push forward with his initiative. He then sent Brad Smith on a speaking tour of the state, presenting talks about traffic safety. Daniel was also able to enlist the help of various businesses throughout the state that gave donations and even lent out human resources to the governor. The governor reached out to several safety commissions throughout the state to bolster his support for the program and unify the messaging. In the first ninety days, the governor's office sent a letter to every county judge to create their own safety committees and support his initiative. Additionally, his office reached out to sheriffs, district attorneys, media personalities, city judges and heads of civic clubs to support the governor in his efforts. The committee would slowly grow to involve the military, due to there being many military bases in the state. Meetings would occur every few weeks at which members would assess what worked and what did not. The Traffic Safety Commission would produce letters, op-eds, news features and other types of messaging for the public. It would also go on to put together a fund of $15 million for rebuilding and improvements of roads and bridges to help alleviate traffic accidents.[98]

One area of focus for the governor's office as well as the people of the area was the Rio Grande Valley, which had experienced a high number of traffic accidents, such as the one in Alamo. The dangers of train crossings were further highlighted on June 27, 1946, when in Harlingen, Texas (a city just thirty miles east of Alamo), a very similar accident occurred at a railroad crossing. The accident occurred as a Missouri Pacific passenger train heading east toward Harlingen collided with a one-and-a-half-ton Chevy truck as it made its way across the tracks from the Adams Gardens packing sheds where the occupants were employed. The workers, like the ones in the Alamo accident, were all Mexican Americans from the town of La Paloma. According to State Highway Patrolman W.G. Poplin, "A number of freight cars, sided on a track nearby, created a blind crossing and neither the engineer nor the driver of the truck would see the other until it was too late." Upon hitting the truck, the train dragged it down the line for 150 feet, "literally tearing it to pieces," which sent the twenty-three people in the back of the truck into the air in every direction. The truck driver, Simon Leal, survived and was sent to the hospital.

Seven people died at the accident site, and one more would die from injuries later in the hospital. In a sad repeat of the Alamo accident, broken and crushed bodies were strewn all along the path of the accident on either side of the tracks. The scene was soon inundated with thousands of people whom the police had to control as they attempted to look at the accident site. There was a much smaller crowd at the hospital made up of friends and family members desperate to hear from a nurse or a doctor about the condition of their loved one or at least to be asked to identify their dead—some closure to help alleviate their anxiety. The hospital itself was notified of the accident shortly after it happened as well as the possibility of multiple fatalities, so staff immediately began to prepare at least twenty beds for a possible influx of patients. There was also a mass call for all available doctors and nurses to come in and lend a hand.[99] This incident had several other repeats throughout the state, but nothing would come close to what had taken place in Alamo. However, this was the reason the traffic program was welcomed in the Valley so that they could find a solution to alleviate these types of fatalities. Farm working and all associated industries, along with the lack of car ownership by many of the workers and the use of trains to connect to national markets throughout the Valley, made a recipe for the frequency of these types of collisions that resulted in multiple casualties.

The Alamo accident, as tragic as it was, did influence many policy decisions throughout the state. Its inclusion as part of the research of the traffic program demonstrates its power as a story and the sheer cost of human life that allowed it to call attention to the dangers of railroad crossings and traffic safety in general. Indeed, according to former Alamo mayor Rudy Villarreal, who was six years old at the time of the accident, after the tragedy, "a lot of truckers had to buy vans to transport their workers to the fields, they didn't want [it] to happen again." So, in one respect, there were changes that came immediately after the accident. However, traffic/train safety is something that continues to be explored and reexamined to this day.

PART IV

REMEMBRANCE

PRESERVING THE STORY

W hat follows is a reflection on how different people in the Rio Grande Valley worked to preserve the story of the Alamo train crash. This was truly the work of the community, who wanted this story to be told and remembered for generations to come.

Besides the memorial held at the Alamo City Park and all the funerals held in Hidalgo and Starr Counties, there was another method by which the story of the tragedy in Alamo was transmitted to the public, and that is the Mexican/Mexican American tradition of the *corrido*. According to Dr. Celestino Fernandez, a corrido is

> *a descriptive narrative, a running account that is written in verse, like poetry, that is put to music. In other words, corridos are stories sung in poetic form and to simple music, much like ballads. The genre originated in Mexico but has become a source of popular expression throughout the nation, and today it is known and performed wherever Mexicans or Mexican Americans reside, including throughout the United States in particular the U.S.-Mexico border region.*[100]

For Mexicans, especially in the United States, the corrido played a vital role in communicating cultural stories, important events and people, as well as the news of the day. Throughout this book, we have cited English-language American newspapers that in a sense would spend most of their

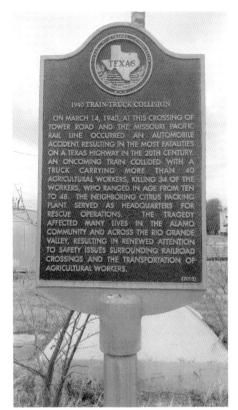 

Left: The historical marker dedicated to the accident. *Courtesy of Juan Carmona.*

Right: The historical marker and flagpole at Landmark Food Truck Park. *Courtesy of Juan Carmona.*

time reporting on events and writing from the perspective of the Anglo, English-speaking community, mostly leaving out the concerns of Mexican Americans. Even if they spoke English, they would rarely see a story that had direct relevance to their community.

Corridos, on the other hand, were written for the Mexican American community, and they became the true voice of the people. The most famous one, "The Ballad of Gregorio Cortez," has been analyzed by Dr. Americo Paredes. This song tells the story of Gregorio Cortez, a small rancher who through a mistranslation of the word *yegua* (female horse) was accused of horse theft. The local sheriff shot Cortez's brother, and Gregorio shot the sheriff before he himself could be killed. This led to one of the largest manhunts in Texas history, in which Cortez constantly evaded the Texas

Rangers, turning him into a folk hero. The most popular version of this corrido has been recorded by Ramon Ayala.

Corridos also served to inform the community of recent events in both Mexico and the United States. According to Dr. Fernandez:

> *Much like the editorial page of the local newspaper, the corrido takes a topic of importance and accurately (mostly) and poetically documents the essential points, interprets them (often through a moral lens), provides commentary, and may offer advice or recommendations. However, the corrido always takes the point of view of the working class; it is from this perspective that an issue is documented, analyzed, and interpreted. In a world in which common people have little economic or political power and influence, cultural expressions such as corridos play an important role in amplifying the voice of El Pueblo.*[101]

There were individuals and groups who would take breaking news stories and overnight create a corrido, record it and hand it over to Spanish-language radio for the public to listen to in the morning on their way to work. This became one major aspect of the lives of Mexican Americans, and the Alamo train crash was no different.

A song was produced within days of the accident and was sold to the community both in records and music sheets for local musicians. Young children would stand at street corners in towns throughout the Valley selling sheets of the corrido for ten cents and an album for one dollar. It was through this method that cafés, restaurants and cantinas shared the story of the tragedy with the wider public. This was not the only story that was shared this way, and one could do decent business in publishing and producing these stories either as a record producer, songwriter or musician. Let us now reflect on individual contributions to the maintenance of this story.

RICK DIAZ

Rick Diaz, a figure whom many Valley natives have regarded as a prominent one in RGV journalism and culture, contributed to the remembrance and commemoration of the Alamo train-truck crash through his reporting. As a student at Pan American University, Diaz was going to school part time and working nights at Channel 5, starting his iconic career at KRGV, the Valley's most-watched news station. Ironically, KRGV is the station at which

State commemorates crash location

By DULCINEA CUELLAR
The Monitor

ALAMO — Espirrion Vera sat in his wheelchair Saturday and watched as a Texas historical marker was placed near the site of the deadliest vehicle accident in the state's history. It was a truck-train wreck that he and only a few others survived 60 years ago.

The frail old man is a stark contrast to the robust 21-year-old he was at the time of the accident.

"You just have to go on," he said. "I lost many friends and family during that accident. I was just lucky."

Vera, 82, walked away from the accident with only a cuts and bruises. He said he still has terrible dreams about the deadly scene, but has learned to cope.

See MARKER page 10B

The *Monitor*'s coverage of the historical marker dedication ceremony. *Courtesy of the City of Alamo Museum.*

previously mentioned reporter Brad Smith, who was on the scene of the crash in 1940, worked as general manager. Throughout his career, Diaz created a news segment that focused on the culture, community and history of the Rio Grande Valley, "Con Mi Gente." "Con Mi Gente" released a story in 2002, approximately sixty-two years after the Alamo train-truck crash, that highlighted the untold stories of the surviving family members of the families affected by the accident. It was Diaz's documentation of the family testimonies that allowed us to further our research and create a focus on the personal narratives of the affected families.

He came to know this story when he was passing by the current location of the Alamo train-truck crash historical marker at the corner of Business 83 and Tower Road. He saw the historical marker, and as a person interested in history, it sparked an interest. He began to reach out to some personal friends from Rio Grande City, starting him on the journey of officially documenting the testimonies of families affected by the crash. Diaz was profoundly affected by the traumatic stories that he was able to document through his outreach. One of the first impactful realizations that Diaz came to was that this accident did not affect only those who had perished but also the surviving family members and descendants of the families, which was not just a couple families but various and extensive family trees. One of the stories that stood out most to him was that some workers, who were parents or children themselves, lost parents and most of their family, making them orphans who would succumb not only to the trauma they would endure as orphans but through the PTSD that manifested itself after the crash. Some surviving relatives began to tattoo their initials onto their arms because they feared being involved in a crash as devastating as the Alamo train-truck crash, when it took so long for their loved ones' bodies to be identified. Secondly, Diaz concluded that the trauma that these surviving relatives lived through extended into their teenage and adult lives, as some had to drop out of school to work and, in some instances, had to work as children to be fed by their foster families. Although many of the affected families sued the railroad company for the damages and trauma caused by the accident, many never received any settlement money, making the trauma not only psychological but financial as well. Most importantly, Diaz emphasized that fieldwork was the way of life for many Mexican American families and sustained the livelihood of these families, and for it to be taken in a "split-second" was heartbreaking because it left a legacy of struggle that needs to be remembered, not only as Valley history but as Mexican American history.[102]

ALEX OYOQUE

Alex Oyoque, current director of the Alamo Museum, summarizes the events that Alamo has had into two important categories: the Alamo train-truck crash and the Alamo bank robbery, two stories that have gone down in Alamo history and have a legacy of infamy. Oyoque, a Reynosa-born Houston native, began his career in graphic design at Centro de Estudios Superiores de Monterrey and worked at the International Museum of Art and Science in McAllen, Texas, from 1992 to 2008, with his last position as facilities director. Oyoque's career at the Alamo Museum began as a volunteering curator and then as museum director starting in 2017. As the Alamo Museum was created, and as Oyoque's career grew with it, one of the main focuses was keeping the museum as a place that would represent and be for the community, while still owned by the city. This is one of the reasons why the Alamo train-truck crash became a permanent exhibit at the Alamo Museum, as it is so valuable and relevant to the community that the museum is intended to serve. Along with this perspective, Oyoque also provided his input on what happened in the seconds leading up to the train-truck crash. In Oyoque's understanding, although the passenger window was broken and covered, obstructing the driver's view of his passenger side mirror, which would have provided a direct view of the train running parallel just beside him, there should have been some way Jose Ramon knew there was a train traveling westbound alongside him. With this in mind, Oyoque rationalizes that there could have been a moment in which Ramon felt he could make it across the tracks. But because of

Alex Oyoque, director of the City of Alamo Museum, in front of the museum display of the accident. *Courtesy of Juan Carmona.*

the standard gear system on the 1937 International, in order to make a right turn, depending on the weight the truck is carrying, you have to turn the clutch all the way in and change the gear, and restart on first gear or continue with the existing momentum and go into second. If, in the seconds leading to the collision, Ramon could not adjust the momentum according to the weight the truck was carrying, which varies due to the forty-some passengers and their work gear, then it would make sense that he was aware of the train and thought he could possibly cross the tracks, but due to the ill-timed gear malfunction, he was not able to. Nonetheless, these theories are rooted in the passed-down stories of Alamo and the Rio Grande Valley, making it a story for the community to uphold.[103]

TRINO MEDINA

Trino Medina from the Alamo Lions Club pointed out that the act of keeping the story of the Alamo train-truck crash relevant is especially important not just for the victims of the accident itself but for their families, as well as anyone with a background in farmwork or the descendants of Mexican American farmworkers. The Alamo Lions Club focuses much of its work on civic duties and assisting the community. The Lions Club's primary role in the commemoration of the event began when one of the members saw the landmark and decided to actively search for the descendants of the victims and affected families. The tradition of storytelling has kept this accident and the victims' memories alive for so long that much of the information and contact efforts were through word of mouth; as the community is tightknit and the historical memory of the accident was kept alive, they were able to find people quite easily. This has turned into a yearly event that everyone connected to the accident is invited to attend.[104]

DIANA MARTINEZ

An Alamo native, Mayor Diana Martinez understands the importance of the stories passed down through generations and upheld in small, tightly rooted communities like Alamo. Mayor Martinez is the daughter of Guadalupe and Herlinda Martinez and recounts that in 1950s Alamo, it was the norm for doctors to make house visits and deliver children in the homes of pregnant mothers. So it was for Mayor Martinez, who was born in a three-bedroom house that acted as a home for herself and her five brothers. The old streets and neighborhoods of Alamo raised various professionals like Mayor Martinez, including Dr. Stephen Brown, District Judge Fernando Mancias and even the Alamo police chief, who lived down the street from Mayor Martinez in the area of Citrus and Seventh. Mayor Martinez included that the area north of the railroad tracks, which would be the area where many of the mentioned individuals grew up, was considered the "Mexicano" side, whereas the south part of town was considered the "Americano" side. The significance of the tracks in this story not only pertains to the crash itself, but it also served as a physical border between class and race groups. This is the case for many Valley towns, such as Weslaco and Donna; the farther you get from the tracks, the bigger the increase in wealth, as the infrastructure and quality of homes change drastically.

Mayor Martinez points out that many of the original and wooden frame homes were those nearest to the tracks, as the town usually grew out from there. Mayor Martinez can now proudly describe the improvements that Alamo and her own family have seen, as Acacia Street used to be all caliche and is now paved, along with the introduction of new businesses, better infrastructure and subdivisions all throughout Alamo. As a young girl, Mayor Martinez recalls her neighborhood and the businesses around it as an area that was made for them, by them. Acacia Street, for example, provided the north side of the tracks with an area to buy and sell. School for children on the north side of the tracks was also a unique experience, as many Mexican American children would have to contribute to their family income by working, whether in their parents' businesses or, most commonly, through fieldwork. Mayor Martinez, for instance, remembers picking cotton or tomatoes. The pattern of Mexican American children working in the fields is something that many Valley natives of Mexican descent can vouch for, and even if they have not experienced fieldwork personally, the stories and experiences of a Mexican American farmworker permeate through families through the tradition of storytelling.[105]

Juan Carmona's Reflections

This project began during the year in which school was being conducted online via a series of Zoom meetings or Google Meets due to COVID-19. I am a social studies teacher in Donna, Texas, and every year, I have found different local history topics for students in my Mexican American Studies class to engage in and produce some sort of project. These projects have been oral histories, presentations at conferences and videos.

The summer before the school year began, I was brainstorming how I could facilitate a project via an online class. Then came one day in July when I was driving home (I was raised in Donna but had recently moved to Alamo) and was stuck in traffic at the intersection of Tower Road and Business Highway 83. Waiting at the light for what seemed like an eternity, I happened to glance to the right (to the west). I saw a historical marker just off the road. It was too far away for me to read, but the one set of words I was able to see was "train crash." I became very curious and immediately drove home and went straight to my computer and searched for information on a train crash, and that's when I came across the story of what happened on March 14, 1940.

My journey exploring the topic brought me to the City of Alamo Museum and Alex Oyoque. The museum had an exhibit that was centered on the accident, with samples of newspaper headlines from across the country, in a demonstration of how big the story was for its time. Oyoque was very generous with his time and knowledge of what happened that tragic day.

The students who assisted with interviews at the accident commemoration ceremony (2022). *From left to right:* Clarissa Rodriguez, Daphne Baez, Danna Baez, Taylor Seaver, Juan Carmona, Nicholle Moreno and Cesar Zamora. *Courtesy of Juan Carmona.*

He went as far as opening the museum for me (it was closed to the general public because of COVID) so that I could see the exhibit and the museum archives. As I learned more, the idea came to me of making a podcast about the incident with my class. I had recently heard a podcast done by a teacher and her middle school students, and I thought that this could be something that my students could certainly do as well.

I waited for the school year to begin and presented it to my Mexican American Studies students, who were excited to do it. I knew that we could work together using a shared drive to house all our research. This allowed me to have students work on different aspects of the stories and dig through the research to help write different parts of the script. I picked one day for the class to meet with Oyoque via Google Meet, during which he could present his knowledge of the topic, as well as answer any student questions. We were also placed in contact with members of the Ramon family via one of Donna High School's art teachers, Vicky Avila, who was related to the Ramons. The family guided us in telling our story by sharing family history, documents and essays on their history. We even included Nick Ramon's knowledge of the incident in one of the podcast episodes. We ended up producing four main episodes and one bonus episode that features Oyoque's online visit with the class. However, I continued to receive and discover more and more documents and interviews, which led to me deciding that this was worthy of a book treatment. Additionally, my coauthor, Taylor Seaver, who narrated the podcast, was graduating and majoring in history and became super invested in the project because she came from a family of farmworkers. Consequently, I asked her to join me in writing this book, and so we spent the next year and a half completing research on this project.

One of the biggest obstacles we came across when we reexamined the newspaper articles and documentation that were associated with the historical marker was that there was no accurate list of who perished in the accident. Different newspapers at the time had different lists. In reviewing the documentation, we came to the realization that this was due to errors in spelling and perhaps a misunderstanding of spellings on the reporters' behalf (Spanish names copied down by Anglo journalists). We then began the hunt to correct the names and provide the community with an accurate list of those who lost their lives. Due to the chaos, there were reports that some wandered away from the accident scene and the same issues of incorrect names being published. We even found that because of misspellings, some people were on the same list more than once.

We went on to create multiple lists by different sources and were able to narrow down some of what we had, but there was still no accurate list. We had heard via former KRGV reporter Rick Diaz that there is a cemetery in Starr County (on the western border of Hidalgo County) where a large group of victims of the accident was buried. We decided to take a trip to the newly incorporated city of Escobares, where the cemetery was located. We began to make a concentric circle around the graveyard, and after almost an hour, we were able to find only a few names. We knew from what Diaz told us and some news footage that there was a row of graves that lay next to each other, but we had not found it. As we walked back to the car, for some reason, something told me to turn to my left. I went in that direction, and there they were. We took it as a sign that they wanted to have their story told.

We were able to use the names on their headstones to clarify spelling and ages. This was not the complete list, but it did help us clear up some of the names. We then turned to death records and sorted by the day of the accident and three days after (because not everyone died that day) and looked for cause or place of death. Not all records contained the cause of death as an accident, so we went by injuries and cross-referenced with what and who we were looking for. We were finally able to come up with an accurate list of the twenty-nine people who lost their lives from the collision. This was our first big milestone and allowed us to move on to search out family members and witnesses to the accident.

To find more people to interview, we turned to social media posts and fliers. This brought some responses that we have used in this book. However, there were a few people who helped us to reach out to people and provided us with names and numbers. These include Alex Oyoque, Alamo mayor Diana Martinez and former Alamo city commissioner and businessman Roy Landa. Mayor Martinez comes from one of the oldest families of Alamo and was able to reach out to friends to find us people to talk to, and through

Top: At the accident commemoration ceremony in 2022, the authors donated an official list of the dead from the accident to the City of Alamo Museum. At the forefront, from left to right, are Alex Oyoque, Taylor Seaver and Juan Carmona. *Courtesy of Larissa Gonzales.*

Bottom: The invocation during the accident commemoration ceremony in 2022. *Courtesy of Larissa Gonzales.*

his connections, Landa was able to connect us with city officials and other members of the community. As we did our research and conducted these interviews, it became obvious that the community of Alamo was heavily invested in telling this story and commemorating the event.

The historical marker that I encountered was displayed in the year 2000. There had been one attempt to establish a marker ten years before, but it met with some opposition when a family member rejected it. In 2000, the community came out to commemorate the tragedy, and on hand were witnesses to the accident, including the Alamo former fire chief Rolando Espinoza and families connected to the tragedy. In 2022, we worked with the city, the local Lions Club and Landa to organize an event to not only memorialize the tragedy but also seek out more people to talk to for this book. We also planned to donate a sign that we made with the accurate list of those who perished in the accident to the City of Alamo Museum.

It was a warm and windy evening, yet still very sunny. There was a large crowd in attendance. Ms. Alamo and her court were also in attendance. Additionally, the mayor, members of the city council, a state representative, Hidalgo County Judge Cortez and members of the Lions Club sponsored the event. It was so windy that we decided not to use the stand for the poster with the names. I had several of my students in attendance: Danna and Daphne Baez, Cesar Zamora, Nicholle Moreno and Clarissa Rodriguez. I asked Larissa Gonzalez, a member of the podcast I host—*Mi Valle Mi Vida*, about the history and culture of the valley—to take pictures and film the ceremony for a YouTube video. There were also members of the media present who did a news piece on it and interviewed several people, including myself.

The ceremony was led by the head of the Alamo Lions Club, Trino Medina. The different dignitaries, including Judge Cortez and the local parish priest, gave speeches talking about the accident and its impact. Taylor and I were the last ones to speak. I spoke a little bit about why I began to research the accident, the podcast my students did and the upcoming book. I then introduced Taylor, and she spoke about why she wanted to continue the project and become a history major. When we were done talking, I presented to the city a poster with the official list of those who perished in the accident. Daphne brought it to the stage and handed it to Trino Medina, who held it for us as we got it to Alex Oyoque. Alex thanked us for the poster and for promising to donate all our research to the museum for posterity. We then ended by announcing that if anyone was willing to sit down and be interviewed, Taylor and my students would be available to record them.

As soon as it was over, everyone was invited to take some yellow flowers from a table that was set up next to the stage and lay them down at the historical marker. Taylor and I made our way off the stage and were immediately inundated by different people wanting to share their stories, from a woman whose father helped pick up the dead and lived traumatized by it to the son of a survivor who also lived his life affected by the horrendous accident. I looked for the students for help and initially could not see them.

I soon realized that they had gone to pay their respects by leaving flowers on the historical marker.

As they came back, I assigned them to get multiple interviews. Danna and her sister Daphne interviewed Trino Medina. Cesar and Nicholle interviewed the son of the survivor, who broke down crying during the interview. Taylor went off to interview the woman whose father helped pick up the body parts. I sat down to interview Jose Ramon Jr., a son of the truck driver, and was joined by Danna and Daphne. He was soon joined by his son as well. We paused for a moment and regrouped to see which interviews everyone had gotten, and then we went on to interview Israel Ramon, a grandson of the driver. It was the last interview of the day, and we gathered afterward for a quick debrief. All in all, I was expecting to either have very few people to interview or a lot. I am glad it was a lot, and each of them thanked us for preserving the story. It was a little hectic, but I am glad it all worked out. I was pleasantly surprised by how many people showed up to the ceremony and by the leads we received that we were able to act on so that we could tell a more complete story.

ROY LANDA JR.

When one makes their way to the site of the accident, one will come along a food truck park called the Landmark on Tower. It is an open-air park with artificial grass, swing set tables, a stage and a series of food trucks selling a variety of different foods. There is a small indoor building that sells brick-oven pizza and wings. The white walls on either side of the entrance doors contain the signatures of bands and patrons who have stopped by or played at the venue in black marker. It is a family- and pet-friendly venue that also hosts local vendors to sell their merchandise on tables set up all around the sides. The location has become a place that draws locals and those from the surrounding communities to meet, listen to music, enjoy a variety of foods and enjoy the cool night air, which is exactly what the owner envisioned when he first looked to purchase the property.

Roy Landa Jr. is a native of the city of Alamo and a business owner, owning several other properties, a home health service and a nursing school. He grew up with a strong sense of history and community. When he purchased the land where the Landmark is, he also acquired the surrounding building, which includes a warehouse that used to be owned by the Crest Fruit Company. Crest Fruit was a major job provider for the city of Alamo and the

Crest Fruit Company. *Courtesy of the City of Alamo Museum.*

surrounding cities. Landa had a large part of his family work with Crest, as did many of the older families of the city. So, to own and preserve its former buildings means a lot to Landa. During his interview, he pointed out the inside part of the Landmark was the office area for the nearby warehouse. He also related that shortly after he opened the park, he saw a woman taking a picture of herself in the dining area, pointing out to her friends that "this was where my office used to be." This is a demonstration of how Crest Fruit and its buildings are deeply interconnected to the citizens of Alamo.

In fact, Roy Landa explained that he wanted to keep the outside structure and main walls intact when he purchased the building. His acquisition of the building came at the height of the COVID-19 pandemic, and his initial thought was to create a community center with several study rooms that had free access to Wi-Fi for the local students to use to continue their studies. However, as he was finally able to start renovations on the school, the cellphone companies and internet providers stepped up to fill in the gaps for students who needed access to the internet to attend online classes and complete their assignments. Nonetheless, he still wanted to have a

This page: Inside the
Crest Fruit packing
plant. *Courtesy of
Roy Landa.*

space for the community to gather, and thus the idea for the Landmark was conceived.

Landa's love for the community has been a major driver in his life. He served as Alamo city commissioner in 2007 and was mentored by a man synonymous with the history and development of Alamo, Rudy Villareal. Villarreal was six years old when the train accident occurred. In an interview during a commemoration ceremony for the accident, he described that he heard the loud crash and explosion from the accident and tried to leave school to see what had happened, but his teacher did not allow him to leave the classroom. Villarreal would go on to lead efforts in the city to commemorate the accident and its impact on the community. Being part of one of the older families that reside in the city, Villarreal was well connected within the community and knew most people by name. Landa describes campaigning with Villarreal and his recall of people's names and telephone numbers; he would hear a name and rattle off their number, all from memory. It was in working with the former mayor and being part of the remembrance ceremony of the accident that Roy Landa would come to recognize the importance of this tragic event to his community.

The historical marker commemorating the accident sits at the southern border of his property, and he has improved public access to the property. The initial land on which the marker was placed was almost like a small grassy hill. If one were to stand in front and read it, one would be standing

Landmark Food Truck Park, whose location is adjacent to the accident site. *Courtesy of Juan Carmona.*

on uneven ground. This made it inaccessible for older or wheelchair-bound residents who may wish to view it. Roy Landa decided to do something about it and laid a concrete square around the area of the marker so people could stand evenly in front of the marker to read it. Additionally, he laid a concrete pathway from the parking lot to the marker, allowing for wheelchair access, as well as an easy, even path for all to make their way. He plans to cast light directly on the marker for night viewing.

Landa continues to be one of the many citizens of Alamo who work to ensure that the memory of this accident is not forgotten. In 2022, with his business fully up and running, he offered the location to the city to hold a large commemoration ceremony, during which many of the interviews used in the book were recorded. He plans to support this commemoration annually. He sees this as part of his responsibility as owner and member of the community. To this day, many who patronize his establishment come for the food and music and get a dose of the history of the location, the Crest Fruit Company and the Alamo train crash of 1940. He accomplished what he set out to do when he purchased the land: provide a place for the community to gather, stay close and bond.[106]

THE OTHER SIDE OF THE ACCIDENT

According to the Federal Railroad Administration Office of Safety Analysis, deaths from railroad accidents have been approximately eight hundred per year for the last four years.[107] This is despite the numerous changes that have been implemented over the past decades because of accidents like the one in Alamo. One can travel around the country and see flashing lights and barriers that come down to prevent vehicles from crossing the railroad, as well as continuous use of loud horns as trains make their way through cities and residential neighborhoods.

One aspect of this story that we have not examined is the impact on the men who were working on the train that collided with Ramon's vehicle. In an interview with the magazine *Popular Mechanics*, Kim David, a train conductor with over four decades of experience, stated, "About 90 percent of the time when a railroad incident is reported, they never mention if the train crew is ok. The reporters are only thinking of half the equation."[108] Statistics show that over half the engineers currently in service have been involved in fatal accidents, most of which are not the fault of the engineer but the actions of others, for simple physics dictates that a train weighing tons, due to not only its makeup but its cargo as well, cannot stop on a dime. These men at the front can see an accident going to happen but can do absolutely nothing to delay the inevitable. For, even though they can see an object or person in the distance and they pull the brakes, it will still take hundreds of yards to come to a complete stop, and that often means whatever they hit they will destroy. If one looks at the accident in Alamo, even that train that was only several cars still took over 750 yards to come to a complete stop, despite dragging Ramon's truck with it.

What does this mean for the engineers, brakemen and others in the front of the train? They have front-row seats to an unpreventable tragedy. They know and see it coming moments before the actual collision. Another engineer employed with Amtrak described this: "They know it's coming, hear the crunch, see the gore, and wonder: Could they have made a difference? But there's not a damn thing you can do."[109] To add fuel to the emotional damage suffered by train engineers, for years, up until the late 1980s, the train companies would force the train crew to clean up after an accident. Then they were supposed to go right back to work, as though nothing had happened.[110] Even though that practice came to an end, engineers are still mandated to remain with their train after an accident occurs and help with the investigation as to what occurred, which can lead them to observe some truly horrible scenes that linger in their minds for years. Dom Fruci related, "You have to get used to the smell. There's a scent to the blood. People don't know until they actually see it, how bad it really is." He went on to say, "You feel like a murderer. You feel responsible."[111]

For decades, the Alamo train men men carried this emotional trauma with them, trying to keep working in their chosen field and provide for their families, but the emotional toll would lead to many of these engineers being diagnosed with post-traumatic stress disorder (PTSD). In response to the mental health needs of railroad employees in 2008, Congress passed the Railway Safety Improvement Act. This act was an immense overhaul of safety standards of the rail industry, and as part of making our railways safe, they also included a provision addressing the mental health of railroad workers. In Section 410 there is a "Critical Incident Stress Plan" that contains the following provisions:

(a) IN GENERAL.—The Secretary of Transportation, in consultation with the Secretary of Labor and the Secretary of Health and Human Services, as appropriate, shall require each Class I railroad carrier, each intercity passenger railroad carrier, and each commuter railroad carrier to develop and submit for approval to the Secretary a critical incident stress plan that provides for debriefing, counseling, guidance, and other appropriate support services to be offered to an employee affected by a critical incident.
(b) PLAN REQUIREMENTS.—Each such plan shall include provisions for—

(1) relieving an employee who was involved in a critical incident of his or her duties for the balance of the duty tour, following any actions necessary for the safety of persons and contemporaneous documentation of the incident.

(2) upon the employee's request, relieving an employee who witnessed a critical incident of his or her duties following any actions necessary for the safety of persons and contemporaneous documentation of the incident; and

(3) providing such leave from normal duties as may be necessary and reasonable to receive preventive services, treatment, or both, related to the incident.

(c) SECRETARY TO DEFINE WHAT CONSTITUTES A CRITICAL INCIDENT.—Within 30 days after the date of enactment of this Act, the Secretary shall initiate a rulemaking proceeding to define the term "critical incident" for the purposes of this section.[112]

This effort by the United States Congress was a reaction to a growing number of concerns regarding railroad safety, especially the usually overlooked topic of the mental health of railroad employees who were in a sense suffering in silence. Engineers and other employees have attested to the fact that for years they worked in an environment that promoted a machismo culture in which they were just supposed to tough it out and keep working, but over time, this can certainly take an emotional toll. Early in the 1990s, some rail employees decided to create an emergency response team called Crisis Assistance Response and Engagement (CARE) that would respond to accidents and counsel those employees involved in the incident. Congress's passage of the Rail Safety Program reflects the awareness of the need for organizations such as CARE to respond to the needs of railway employees.

Consequently, when reflecting on the graphic nature of the accident and the carnage of the scene, one should keep in mind those who were working in the train's engine. Like all engineers and other employees who watch the tracks before them, they observed what was just before them and knew consciously that they could not stop the train in time to not collide with the object on the tracks. Therefore, they are powerless firsthand witnesses to all manner of calamity, including what happened in March 1940.

AFTERWORD

BY TAYLOR SEAVER

The experiences of farmworkers are not heard enough, which is why documenting the Alamo train-truck crash is so vital to Rio Grande Valley history. This story alone does not detail the daily sacrifices and hardships that Mexican farmworkers endured and continue to endure. By including the stories of my grandparents and mother, I hope to illustrate how difficult fieldwork was, because it was not an "unskilled" job; it was a career that many went into to uphold their livelihood and has lasted as a legacy for many Rio Grande Valley families.

I was raised on stories of fieldwork, the migrating circuit and childhood adventures that my mom experienced as a young Mexican migrant farmworker. Every night before going to bed, I would request a new story to be told to me, because to a young child, the imagery of apple orchards and strawberry fields sounded like pure fun. But as I became older, the stories that I was told would eventually unearth more negative feelings and reveal the ugly side of farmwork as a Mexican. The romanticized stories I heard as a young child were soon reshaped with added details. I began to realize that picking berries and vegetables would be fun if it was for your own enjoyment, but not when your livelihood depended on it and there was no place to call home, at least for more than a few months. Even so, the thought of never being in one place too long sounded like an adventure, and that is what my mom, as the oldest daughter, had to do for her younger siblings. Romanticizing fieldwork, inadequate living situations and poor pay were some things that the children of migrant farmworkers had to do to live through what is now categorized

Left: Members of Taylor Seaver's family. Jose Hector De La Fuente (Taylor's grandfather) and Amelia Emma Villareal De La Fuente (Taylor's grandmother). *Courtesy of Taylor Seaver.*

Opposite: Members of Taylor Seaver's family. Jose Hector De La Fuente (Taylor's grandfather) holding Melissa De La Fuente (Taylor's mother). *Courtesy of Taylor Seaver.*

as a valid childhood trauma. One story that changed the course of these bedtime stories is when my grandmother told me that because she and the other workers would pick raspberries, strawberries and blackberries, their hands became stained red, blue or purple by berry juice. When the workers would make stops at the local small stores or gas stations, the white cashiers would wince at the sight of the stained hands. My grandmother was fed up with this treatment, so when a cashier would not take the money from her stained working hands, my grandmother remarked, "What? Is my money not good enough for you?" For a lot of my life, I never understood how my grandmother could be so outspoken, but as I reflect on the stories I grew up with, I realize it was because she was forced to be outspoken because many of her experiences were uncomfortable.

The living situation of farmworkers was never definite, as the job sometimes required families to be uprooted and travel around the United

States. Whenever work was offered and needed, even for the farmworkers that did not necessarily migrate, the pay was still not enough to fully sustain family life. My grandfather was what could be considered in this context a mayordomo or supervisor. He came to the United States from Nuevo Leon when his mother remarried; his stepfather offered my then-teenage grandfather a job in the fields, which he took and would make his career and passion until the day he passed. As his career progressed, he was able to invest in some large produce-holding trucks that were used to drive workers around the United States, in the same way that Jose Ramon traveled with his sons and workers. It was dangerous, but it was the main way of transportation for field workers. Upon arriving at various "migrant camps" around the United States, my grandmother, who could speak fluent English, would be the one to negotiate with the Anglo ranch or farm owner about where the "people" or workers would stay for the season. Oftentimes, the migrant camp would be structured with no running water, covered windows or even floors, but this was livable in comparison to the barns that some farm and ranch owners would offer as living quarters. My mom recalls being a child working up north, sleeping in a barn along with her family and other working families, and waking up in the middle of the night to noises. When she looked up, she saw the barn ceiling filled with bats. In other living situations, it was just as inhumane and dangerous. These northern states were starkly different from the Rio Grande Valley because of the thick forests, cold nights and extreme winters, as well as the possibility of wolves and bears lurking around the migrant campsites. These factors did not inhibit Mexican farmworkers from getting the job done because of their strong work ethic. Like the workers in Jose Ramon's truck, their work ethic was their reputation.

While researching and writing about the Alamo train-truck crash of 1940, I couldn't help but find similarities between the sacrifice the workers made that day and the many sacrifices farmworkers like my grandparents had to make throughout their lives. I didn't go to kindergarten, so my daily lessons were with my grandparents, who were still not retired from their careers in farmwork, although as older laborers, they mainly did the payroll and supervising jobs, not literal fieldwork. Since my grandparents could not leave me at home, I had to go with them to the produce sheds. I can still smell and taste the intense aroma of freshly picked carrots and onions that were being packaged by workers. These sheds were on the outskirts of Valley towns like Weslaco, Alamo and Donna, so to me, it was like my own daily adventure. As I have been able to reflect on these moments, I realized that farm working was literally with my grandparents until the weeks leading up to their passing. Farm working provided them with a career, money to raise a family and the opportunity to make lifelong connections and friendships.

NOTES

Brief History of the Rio Grande Valley and the City of Alamo

1. Scott, *Historical Heritage of the Lower Rio Grande Valley*, 2.
2. Ward, "Hide and Tallow Trade."
3. Foscue, "Land Utilization," 2.
4. *History Detectives*, "Episode 1, 2006: Chisholm Trail, Donna, Texas."
5. Foscue, "Land Utilization," 3.
6. Brannstrom and Neuman, "Inventing the 'Magic Valley,'" 127.
7. *Ireton Ledger*, "Diary of a Delightful Trip," 1.
8. Matthewson, "Additional Society Notes," 2.
9. Montejano, *Anglos and Mexicans*, 78.
10. Alonzo, *Tejano Legacy*, 198–99.
11. Montejano, *Anglos and Mexicans*, 115–17.
12. Castillo, *Celebrating Alamo*, 12.
13. Ibid., 13.
14. Alamo EDC, "Alamo's History."
15. Castillo, *Celebrating Alamo*, 49.
16. Ibid., 64.
17. Ibid.
18. Ibid., 50.
19. Ibid., 72.
20. Ibid., 82.
21. Ibid., 63–65.
22. *Alamo News*, "Money Recovered," 1.

RGV Train History

23. "Pros and Cons of Narrow-Gauge Railways."

24. Allhands, "Lott, Uriah."
25. Knight, "Field Guide to Irrigation," 21–24.

Train Operations

26. Interstate Commerce Commission, "Report of the Director Bureau of Safety."
27. Porterfield interview.
28. Ibid.
29. National Museum of American History: Behring Center, "Riding and Working on the Railroad."
30. Porterfield interview.
31. Kinsella, "Pullman Porters."

The Lives of Farmworkers

32. Ruiz, in *Mexican American Women*, 35.

Ramon Family History

33. Nick Ramon interview
34. Ibid.
35. Ibid.

The Crash

36. Israel Ramon Jr. interview.
37. Ramon, "Family Outline."
38. Monitor, "Memorial," 6.
39. Ramon, "Family Outline."
40. Interstate Commerce Commission, "Report of the Director Bureau of Safety," 2.
41. Ibid., 3.
42. Ibid., 5.
43. *Valley Evening Monitor*, "27 Killed in Valley Crash."
44. Interstate Commerce Commission, "Report of the Director Bureau of Safety," 5.
45. Ibid., 6–7.
46. *Valley Morning Star*, "Eyewitness Accounts Tell of Horror of Alamo Accident."

Eyewitness Statements

47. *Alamo News*, "Truck-Train."
48. *McAllen Monitor*, "Witness," 2.
49. Ibid.
50. Ibid.
51. *Monitor*, "Accident at Alamo," 16A.

52. Ibid.
53. Ibid.
54. *McAllen Monitor*, "Witness," 2.
55. Smith, "Baylor Bus Crash."
56. Danner, "Immortal Ten."
57. Smith, "Alamo Crash," 2.
58. *Valley Morning Star*, "Eyewitness Accounts Tell of Horror."
59. Smith, "Alamo Crash," 3.
60. *Valley Morning Star*, "Eyewitness Accounts Tell of Horror."
61. *McAllen Daily Press*, "Alamo Wreck Picture Brings Smith Honors," 1.
62. Interstate Commerce Commission, "Report of the Director Bureau of Safety," 6–9.

Direct Impacts and Response

63. Donaciano Garza interview.
64. Hinojosa interview.
65. Israel Ramon Jr. interview.
66. Jose Ramon interview.
67. Cortez interview.

The Rosas

68. Alaniz, "Orphan at Seven."

Aftermath

69. *Valley Morning Star*, "3 More Die Thursday."
70. *Delphos Daily Herald*, "23 Killed as Texas Train Strikes Truck," 1.
71. *McAllen Daily Press*, "25 Die," 3.
72. Margaret H. McAllen Memorial Archives, "McAllen Hospital."
73. *Brownsville Herald*, "Eight in Hospital," 2.
74. *Monitor*, "Two Alamo Crash Victims Improve," 1.
75. *Monitor*, "Last Victim Buried in Starr County Area."
76. Maria de Pilar Garza interview.

The Legal System

77. *El Paso Herald*, "Railroad Absolved in Crossing Crash," 8.
78. *Brownsville Herald*, "ICC Rules on Alamo Crash," 2.
79. Roosevelt quoted in "What Is the Good Neighbor Policy?"
80. Library of Congress, "1938: Spanish Speaking People's Congress."
81. *Valley Morning Star-Monitor-Herald*, "Last Victim Is Buried," 2.
82. *Monitor*, "Three Suits Are Filed in Fatal Alamo Crash," 1.
83. Ibid.

84. Ibid.
85. *Valley Morning Star*, "At Least 11 Cases Due in Alamo Wreck," 1.
86. *Monitor*, "Damage Suits Now at $672,000," 3.
87. *Valley Morning Star*, "More Suits Filed," 10.
88. *Valley Morning Star*, "Damage Suit Total Grows," 1.
89. *Valley Morning Star*, "Damage Suits Now $672,000."
90. *Valley Sunday Star-Monitor-Herald*, "Alamo Crash Damage Suit to Be Tried," 2.
91. *Monitor*, "Damage Suits Now at $672,000," 3.
92. *Valley Evening Monitor*, "Alamo Crash Suits Settled for $28,000," 1.

Fundraising Efforts

93. *McAllen Daily Press*, "Alamo Crash Victims to Receive Aid," 1.
94. *Star Monitor Herald*, "Charity Show Receives $124."
95. *Brownsville Herald*, "Theater Helps Crash Victims," 2.
96. *Brownsville Herald*, "Show Nets Crash Victims $320."
97. *Valley Evening Monitor*, "Red Cross Seeks Aid in Supporting Survivors," 1.

Traffic Safety Program

98. Margaret H. McAllen Memorial Archives, "Texas First Traffic Safety Program."
99. *Valley Morning Star*, "All of Victims Not Identified," 2.

Preserving the Story

100. Celestino Fernandez, "What are Corridos and Why Are They So Important," 10, file:///C:/Users/jpcarmona/Downloads/Corridos%20Stories%20of%20the%20People%20Reading.pdf.
101. Fernandez, "Corridos (Mostly True) Stories in Verse and Music," 64.
102. Diaz interview.
103. Oyoque interview.
104. Medina interview.
105. Martinez interview.
106. Landa interview.

The Other Side of the Accident

107. Federal Railroad Administration Office of Safety Analysis, "Total Accidents/Incidents."
108. Orf, "Part of the Job."
109. Lindsay, "Train Accidents' Forgotten Victims."
110. Orf, "Part of the Job."
111. Lindsay, "Train Accidents' Forgotten Victims."
112. 110th Congress, *Federal Rail Safety Improvements*.

BIBLIOGRAPHY

Alamo Economic Development Corporation. "Alamo History: A Glimpse into the Past." www.alamoedc.org/alamos-history-glimpse-past.

Alamo News. "Money Recovered from Alamo Bank Robbery on Saturday." April 27, 1961, 1.

———. "Truck-Train." March 14, 1940, 2.

Alaniz, Christopher. "Orphan at Seven." Personal papers of the Alaniz family.

Allhands, J.L. "Lott, Uriah (1842–1915)." Handbook of Texas Online. www.tshaonline.org/handbook/entries/lott-uriah.

Alonzo, Armando C. *Tejano Legacy: Rancheros and Settlers in South Texas, 1734–1900.* Albuquerque: University of New Mexico Press, 1998.

Brannstrom, Christian, and Matthew Neuman. "Inventing the 'Magic Valley' of South Texas, 1905–1941." *The Geographical Review* (2009).

Brownsville Herald. "Eight in Hospital." March 22, 1940, 1.

———. "Show Nets Crash Victims $320." April 18, 1940.

———. "Theater Helps Crash Victims." April 12, 1940, 2.

Castillo, Fernando. *Celebrating Alamo, Texas Family, and Legacy.* Published by the City of Alamo.

Cortez, Richard Felipe. Interview by Juan Carmona, February 2, 2022.

Danner, Megan. "The Immortal Ten." Waco History. wacohistory.org/items/show/103.

Delphos Daily Herald. "23 Killed as Texas Train Strikes Truck." March 14, 1940, 1.

Diaz, Rick. Interview by Juan Carmona, February 28, 2021.

El Paso Herald. "Railroad Absolved in Crossing Crash." March 19, 1940, 8.

Federal Railroad Administration Office of Safety Analysis. "Total Accidents/Incidents, Jan–Oct 2022." safetydata.fra.dot.gov/officeofsafety/publicsite/summary.aspx.

Fernandez, Celestino. "Corridos (Mostly True) Stories in Verse and Music." *Journal of Folklore and Education* (2021).

Foscue, Edwin J. "Land Utilization in the Lower Rio Grande Valley of Texas." *Economic Geography* (1932).

Garza, Donaciano. Interview by Juan Carmona and Taylor Seaver, February 4, 2022.

Garza, Maria de Pilar. Interview by Taylor Seaver, March 14, 2022.

Hinojosa, Mr. Interview by Taylor Seaver, March 14, 2022.

History Detectives. "Episode 1, 2006: Chisholm Trail Donna, Texas." 2006. www-tc.pbs.org/opb/historydetectives/static/media/transcripts/2011-04-28/401_chisholm.pdf.

Interstate Commerce Commission. "Report of the Director Bureau of Safety: Accident on the Gulf Coast Lines of the Missouri Pacific Lines: Alamo, Texas: March 14, 1940: Investigation No. 2419." Accident Report, 1940.

Ireton Ledger. "Diary of a Delightful Trip to the 'Magic Valley of Texas.'" May 13, 1920, 1.

Kinsella, Lucy. "Pullman Porters: From Servitude to Civil Rights." Chicago Stories WTTW. interactive.wttw.com/a/chicago-stories-pullman-porters.

Knight, Lila. "A Field Guide to Irrigation in the Lower Rio Grande Valley." Texas Department of Transportation: Economic Affairs Division, Historical Studies Branch.

Landa, Roy. Interview by Juan Carmona, February 2, 2023.

Library of Congress. "1938: Spanish Speaking People's Congress." Research Guides. guides.loc.gov/latinx-civil-rights/spanish-speaking-peoples-congress.

Lindsay, Jay. "Train Accidents Forgotten Victims: Conductors, Engineers." *Los Angeles Times*, February 28, 1999. www.latimes.com/archives/la-xpm-1999-feb-28-mn-12504-story.html.

Margaret H. McAllen Memorial Archives, Museum of South Texas History. "Texas First Traffic Safety Program."

Martinez, Diana. Interview by Juan Carmona and Taylor Seaver, February 9, 2022.

Matthewson. "Additional Society Notes." *Wellington Daily News*, February 24, 1919, 2.

McAllen Daily Press. "Alamo Crash Victims to Receive Aid." March 29, 1940, 1.

———. "Alamo Wreck Picture Brings Smith Honors." December 9, 1940, 1.

———. "25 Die." March 14, 1940, 3.

McAllen Monitor. "Witness." March 14, 1940, 2.

Medina, Trino. Interview by Nicholle Moreno and Cesar Zamora, March 14, 2022.

Monitor. "Accident at Alamo Believed to Be Worst of Kind on Texas Records." March 2000, 16A.

———. "Damage Suits Now at $672,000." December 1, 1940, 3.

———. "Last Victim Buried in Starr County Area." March 17, 1940.

———. "Memorial." March 3, 2002, 6.

———. "Three Suits Are Filed in Fatal Crash." March 31, 1940, 1.

———. "Two Alamo Crash Victims Improve." April 4, 1940, 1.

Montejano, David. *Anglos and Mexicans in the Making of Texas, 1836–1986.* Austin: University of Texas Press, 1987.

National Museum of American History: Behring Center. "Riding and Working on the Railroad." americanhistory.si.edu/america-on-the-move/lives-railroad.

110th Congress. *Federal Rail Safety Improvements.* Washington, D.C.: U.S. Congress, 2008.

Orf, Darren. *Popular Mechanics.* "Part of the Job: How Engineers Deal with Death on the Railroad." April 9, 2014. www.popularmechanics.com/technology/infrastructure/a10450/death-on-the-railroad-16675879.

Oyoque, Alex. Interview by Juan Carmona and Taylor Seaver, December 28, 2022.

Porterfield, James. Interview by Juan Carmona and Taylor Seaver, February 7, 2022.

"The Pros and Cons of Narrow Gauge Railways." www.regionen.sachsen.de/en/the-pros-and-cons-of-narrow-gauge-railways-4455.html.

Ramon, Israel, Jr. Interview by Juan Carmona and Taylor Seaver, March 14, 2022.

Ramon, Jose. Interview by Juan Carmona and Taylor Seaver, March 14, 2022.

Ramon, Nick. 2021. "Family Outline." Personal papers.

Ramon, Nick. Interview by Juan Carmona, February 21, 2021.

Roosevelt, Franklin D. "What Is the Good Neighbor Policy." American Historical Association. www.historians.org/about-aha-and-membership/aha-history-and-archives/gi-roundtable-series/pamphlets/em-14-is-the-good-neighbor-policy-a-success-(1945)/what-is-the-good-neighbor-policy.

Ruiz, Vicki. *Mexican American Women, Dress, and Gender: Pachucas, Chicanas, Cholas.* New York: Routledge, 2019.

Scott, Florence Johnson. *Historical Heritage of the Lower Rio Grande Valley.* N.p.: Naylor Press, 1937.

Smith, Brad. "The Alamo Crash." Margaret H. McAllen Memorial Archives, Museum of South Texas History.

———. "Baylor Bus Crash." Margaret H. Mcallen Memorial Archives, Museum of South Texas History.

Star Monitor Herald. "Charity Show Receives $124." March 31, 1940.

Valley Evening Monitor. "Alamo Crash Suits Settled for $28,000." December 2, 1940, 1.

———. "Red Cross Seeks Aid in Supporting Survivors of Alamo Train Accident." April 19, 1940, 1.

———. "27 Killed in Valley Crash." March 15, 1940.

Valley Morning Star. "All of Victims Not Identified." June 26, 1946, 2.

———. "Damage Suit Total Grows." April 26, 1940, 1.

———. "Eyewitness Accounts Tell of Horror of Alamo Accident; Valley Stunned." March 15, 1940.

———. "More Suits Filed." April 3, 1940, 10.

———. "3 More Die Thursday; No Charges Filed." March 15, 1940.

Valley Sunday Star-Monitor-Herald. "Alamo Crash Damage Suit to Be Tried." September 1, 1940, 2.

Ward, Hortense Warner. "Hide and Tallow Trade." Handbook of Texas Online. www.tshaonline.org/handbook/online/articles/dfh01.

ABOUT THE AUTHORS

Juan P. Carmona is a social studies teacher at Donna High School and a dual enrollment history instructor through South Texas College. He graduated with honors from the American Military University with a master's degree in American history and was the recipient of the 2018 James F. Veninga Outstanding Teaching Humanities Award by Humanities Texas. He is a member of the award-winning Refusing to Forget Project and a member of the Hidalgo County Historical Commission. His primary field of research is the history of the South Texas borderlands. He is the author of the book *The Alton Bus Crash*, co-host of the podcast *Mi Valle Mi Vida* and produced a podcast with his Mexican American Studies students called *The Alamo Train Crash of 1940*.

Taylor Seaver De La Fuente is a Rio Grande Valley native from a family of Mexican and Mexican American migrant farmworkers. Her journey in Mexican American studies began in her high school MAS class, taught by Juan Carmona, in which her passion for history collided with her passion for her Chicana heritage. She is a graduate student, studying Mexican American Studies at the University of Texas–Rio Grande Valley. Her research focuses on local and regional history, with current work on the evolution of Mexican American Studies within the RGV and at the UTRGV, as well as research that focuses on the contributions of Chicanx youth in the RGV during the civil rights era. As she continues her research and studies, she hopes to focus on the components that create a Chicanx identity through the intertwined attributes of expressive arts and folk traditions. Her work is motivated and inspired by the lived experiences of the community that encompass cultural resistance and perseverance.